TWO is ENOUGH

A Couple's Guide to
Living Childless by Choice

LAURA S. SCOTT

SEAL PRESS

Two Is Enough
A Couple's Guide to Living Childless by Choice

Copyright © 2009 by Laura S. Scott

Published by
Seal Press
A Member of the Perseus Books Group
1700 Fourth Street
Berkeley, California

Library of Congress Cataloging-in-Publication Data

Scott, Laura S.
 Two is enough : a couple's guide to living childless by choice / Laura
S. Scott.
    p. cm.
 Includes bibliographical references.
 ISBN 978-1-58005-263-4
 1. Childlessness. 2. Childlessness--United States. 3. Parenthood.
I. Title.
 HQ755.8.S366 2009
 306.87--dc22
                                        2009004841

9 8 7 6 5 4 3 2

Cover design by Domini Dragoone
Interior design by Tabitha Lahr
Printed in the United States of America
Distributed by Publishers Group West

For my parents and for my husband, Robert—

my beacons and my anchors.

CONTENTS

INTRODUCTION

The Childless by Choice Project

"So why did you get married if you didn't want kids?" asked the new dad, the husband of one of my friends.

Huh? "Love . . . companionship," I blurted.

His question startled me, rendering me uncharacteristically short of words. I had just spent a year doing research in preparation for what I hoped would be a book and documentary on the childless by choice, but nothing I had read prepared me for this question. He cocked his head and waited for more, his curiosity genuine.

In that moment, I recognized just how strange I must have seemed to him. Here was a person who could not imagine a life without kids trying to understand a person who could not imagine a life *with* kids. I was struggling to find the words to explain why someone would choose a childless marriage, and "love" and "companionship" were all I could come up with. It was the most honest answer I could give, but it clearly did not satisfy him, leaving me with the very distinct feeling that the underlying question was "Is love enough?"

Before I could elaborate, his wife called us to dinner, which she had thoughtfully scheduled between breastfeedings, and we went on to other topics like film and writing, pursuits we all shared. After I left their home that evening, I began thinking of all the other questions that had gone unasked and unanswered:

- Is love enough to sustain a successful union, or are we instinctually or otherwise compelled or obligated to have kids?
- What motivates someone to forgo the experience of parenthood?
- Can couples really find fulfillment and happiness without children?

I could understand why parents might have difficulty wrapping their brains around intentional childlessness. It was strange, even to me. Here I was, a healthy, happily married woman, surrounded by parents and parents-to-be, yet I had never felt a pang of longing for a child. I enjoy spending time with kids and I understand the appeal of children, but I've never wanted one for myself.

Like many of the decisions we make in life, my decision to remain childless was motivated in part by fear—fear of regret. I was afraid to take the risk that I might be a bitter, unhappy, or regretful mom. Given my disinterest in the role of parent, this was a real possibility—particularly when I started hearing from parents who felt compelled to speak out, saying things like "You're lucky not to have kids. They will break your heart."

In my mid-thirties, as I became increasingly comfortable identifying myself as childless by choice, I started hearing comments like these from parents who felt equally comfortable in the presence of a childfree person to share some of their personal turmoil about parenthood. At first I was shocked, since some of the people who were sharing with me were women and men I knew who had raised "good" children, who were seemingly happy and capable parents. Soon, I became accustomed to being pulled into corners, lowered voices imploring, "Please don't share this with anyone. . . . "

I came away from those hushed confessions feeling like I was privy to the best-kept secret in the world: A surprising number of outwardly happy parents have misgivings or regrets about parenthood. At first I felt justified in my choice to remain childless, but mostly I felt sad, especially for those men and women who told me they'd never imagined they had the choice *not* to be a parent. I was left to wonder if these feelings came from their difficult experiences as parents, or if they were regretful because they didn't feel they'd had a choice in the matter.

On the other side of the spectrum, I had many encounters with parents who endorsed parenthood enthusiastically, usually in response to my confession that I was devoid of any maternal feelings. They told me I would change my mind, that "it's different when they're yours." They credited their children with bringing joy and wonder to their lives, and they seemed frustrated or sad about my childfree status because clearly, I didn't get it. I was "missing out" on a whole dimension of experience, the lack of which would leave me less than whole.

Being alternately envied and pitied was bewildering for me. So was the realization that some people believed I had remained childless because I was selfish, immature, lazy, materialistic, or a kid hater—none of which was good, all of which was at odds with how I perceived myself. This disparity between how I was perceived and how I actually felt forced me to question my own ideas about myself and my life. Was I a freak? A slacker? Was I developmentally disabled—in some kind of arrested state, like Peter Pan? Did I have an obligation to procreate?

The assumptions people often make about the voluntarily childless troubled me because they didn't come close to capturing my complex motives. I was not motivated to remain childless because I didn't like kids or because I wanted to spend my money on cars and diamonds instead of cribs and diapers. I was motivated to be childfree because there was so much about my life that I enjoyed and so much that I still wanted to do, experiences that I felt I would have to delay or forgo if I had children. I remained childless because I valued my freedom to do the things I thought I could do well and happily, things I had dreamed of doing all my life.

The fact that parenthood was conspicuously absent from my "ten things to do before I die" list spoke volumes. I had no desire, no longing, to have a child to call my own. Rocking a child to sleep or breastfeeding an infant held no appeal for me, and on the few occasions when I did hold an infant in my arms, I felt awkward and inept. I had decided that Mom was not a role I was well suited for, much the same way I'd determined I would never be a mathematician or a veterinarian.

I had spent very little time pondering my childless status until I found Madelyn Cain's book *The Childless Revolution* at my local Barnes & Noble, which led to a defining moment. Among stories of women who were childless by "choice, chance, or happenstance," I found myself reflected in a small subsection of the choice group Cain had labeled "positively childfree."

It was then, at age forty-three, in the sixteenth year of my intentionally childless marriage, that I realized I was "childfree" and was likely to remain so, given that my egg inventory had reached its "use by" date.

The suggestion that I was part of a defined subset of childless people inspired me to read all I could find on being childfree by choice. Books and articles on the subject were hard to track down, however. Most were dated or out of print, or focused exclusively on the woman's point of view, based on the assumption that motherhood is instinctual and fatherhood is learned. An anomaly in our pronatalist culture, the childless by choice had periodically come under the scrutiny of writers and social scientists, but few had invited the childfree to speak for themselves, outside of the limitations of tabloid sensationalism, academic or scientific inquiry, or the presumption of "deviance."

I realized that someone needed to extend this invitation: to survey the childfree to see if our realities matched the assumptions, and to identify the most compelling motives to remain childless. I also wanted to explore, through interviews, the decision-making processes of childfree couples. And, because I understood that many of us were wary of being judged or analyzed by those who couldn't imagine a life without kids, I decided the person to do this work needed to be intentionally childfree, too.

I embarked on what I came to call the Childless by Choice Project. It was the beginning of a four-year journey of discovery that would ultimately include a literature review, a survey, in-depth video and audio interviews with childfree couples, advocates, demographers, and social scientists throughout North America, and, eventually, this book, and a documentary that's being developed as I write this book.

THE RESEARCH

Before I began researching the Childless by Choice Project, I knew very little about the motives and rationales behind people's choice to remain childless. I also had very little exposure to those who had made this choice.

There were lots of reasons why I didn't want to have children: I was content as a childless person; I valued the time, freedom, and independence I had to pursue my passions; and I loved my childfree marriage and our peaceful and quiet household. But I wondered: Am I alone in this? Why do other people make the choice to remain childless? Is it really a conscious decision, or does it just happen?

These were some of the questions that fueled my research for the Childless by Choice Project. I had two primary objectives for my research and the survey: to determine the most compelling motives to remain childfree, and to better understand the decision-making process of the childless by choice. I suspected their reasons were as complex and varied as my own, beyond the scope of what is too often characterized as simply a "lifestyle choice."

I decided that if I was going to learn anything about this decision making, I would have to survey people who had actually made a choice—who believed they could have had children but had made the decision not to. By focusing the bulk of my inquiries on people who remained childless due to choices they had made, I figured I'd be able to illuminate the decision-making process by concentrating on issues related to personal motivations and preferences, rather than circumstance.

For the purposes of this project, the childless by choice were defined as those who are voluntarily childless, whether they make the decision at age fourteen or age forty. I decided not to include women who had, intentionally or otherwise, postponed childbearing until they were beyond the age at which they could conceivably procreate, even with fertility treatments, and were left to resign themselves to living with the fact that they'd never have children, as they did not actively choose this scenario. I did include some women, however, who had postponed conception or couldn't conceive and felt they had come to terms with the idea of being childless. These women had consciously chosen to remain childless over other viable options that may have led to their having a child. As you will see in Chapter 5, there are women who have tried to have a child and then later decided to stop trying, choosing instead to embrace a childfree life with their partner.

To gather the necessary data, I designed a questionnaire that would feature eighteen motive statements (which are detailed extensively in Chapter 4) and some open-ended and multiple-choice questions relating to motives and decision making. I arrived at these motive statements by first identifying the reasons for remaining childless that were cited most frequently in the literature I had read. I then turned these reasons into motive statements and invited my survey participants to rate them on a scale of 0 to 5, to indicate the degree to which they did or did not identify with the statement (see Appendix B for the questionnaire used in this survey).

I recruited two childless by choice sociologists to assist me in getting the language just right and making sure we had the most common motives covered. I also enlisted Jerry Steinberg, the self-described "founding non-father" of No Kidding!, an international social club for the childfree, to help me find participants. He put me in touch with club leaders in North America, who helped spread the word. I used word of mouth as much as possible, asking friends and acquaintances if they knew of anyone who was childless by choice. These efforts, along with some publicity generated by a newspaper feature article on the Childless by Choice Project, netted 171 qualified, self-identified, voluntarily childless survey respondents ranging in age from twenty-two to sixty-six, 71 percent of whom were female and 29 percent of whom were male.

Since I am a writer, not a statistician, I also recruited statistician and educator Dr. Charles Houston of University Consultants. He helped me analyze the data and, to my relief, reassured me that although my sampling of respondents was not large enough to be representative of the childless by choice, I did have enough respondents for a qualitative survey and enough quality data to do a statistical analysis. This was good news to me because I wanted my research to yield data that was scientifically sound and could be used confidently by others for the purposes of future research, books, articles, and studies on the childless by choice.

As Dr. Houston and I would find upon completing our analysis of the survey data, the Childless by Choice Project participants were compelled to remain childfree based on a combination of motives. Almost all of them identified strongly with at least three of the eighteen motive statements. We also found that when it came to the most compelling motives, men and women were in agreement (see Chapter 4 and Appendix A for more on our findings on gender). The survey data also allowed us to analyze the most compelling motives by age and by decision-making category.

Our analysis yielded some extremely valuable information, resulting in findings that would provide much of the foundation for this work. However, I feared that the statistical analysis of the data generated by the questionnaires alone was not going to be enough to illustrate the complexity and nuances of the decision-making process of the voluntarily childless. Therefore, I supplemented the survey with twenty-eight in-depth interviews with childfree by choice couples and partners. Many highlights from those interviews are included in the chapters that follow. Over two years, I traveled to ten states and two Canadian provinces to do audio and video interviews with people in childfree partnerships. I asked them to elaborate on their motives, decision-making process, lifestyle, and the pros and cons of a childfree partnership.

These interviews with couples were important to me because, from the outset of the project, I felt it was necessary to include men and get their perspective. After all, they are (in many cases) the other half of the decision-making process. Their choices and ideals play an equally valid and important role in establishing the demographic that is the childfree. Many of the published works on the childless by choice have been written for and about women. Those that are tend to focus on the gender-identity aspect of childlessness, asking some variation of the question "How does a woman define herself outside of motherhood?" Within that narrow scope, the influence of the male partner in decision making is often overlooked. In an attempt to avoid that trap, I made it my goal to direct at least 40 percent of my interview questions to the male member of the partnership. I was happy to discover that the men had a lot to say.

These interviews allowed me to flesh out the statistics and identify some of the challenges people face in the course of making this choice. And through these conversations, I came to understand that making this choice is often just one stage in the process. I found people who had moved beyond the assumption of parenthood, who were forging identities in a culture that still holds parenthood as the ideal, and were navigating a pathway that is increasingly acknowledged but not yet fully understood or accepted.

To date, no one has ever conducted a random, large-scale survey of the childless by choice in North America. Most of the surveys on voluntary childlessness, including mine, are described as qualitative rather than quantitative, utilizing self-selected participants (mostly women) in samples too small in number to be representative.

What sets my survey apart from others is the attention given to the decision-making process and the motives and influences that drive that process. Some of the most interesting and valuable information is the qualitative stuff—responses to open-ended questions, which typically resist statistical analysis. The survey was important to me not because it allowed me to break down the childless by choice rationale into a series of percentages or numbers, but because it gave me access to diverse voices and rationales, and the insight I needed to confidently communicate and accurately present the childless by choice perspective.

It is my hope that my efforts will inform or inspire additional exploration and research into the voluntarily childless demographic. As you can imagine, much work remains to be done.

THE CAVEAT

Much of what I have learned through the Childless by Choice Project has been organic, a continuous spiral of questioning, filtering the information through the soil of my own experience and assumptions, and then standing back. I became like a fox on a scent trail, tracking back and forth, going over new ground and old, alternately in the mindset of the hunter and the hunted. Other times, I was simply the amused and delighted observer.

All of these perspectives are offered here. By virtue of my own status and because of the nature of my interactions with the men and women I interviewed, it is impossible for me to present what I have learned in a dispassionate or scientific way. I am childless by choice, and I came to this project with all the biases and the baggage we bring to any journey. I can speak only for myself and for those who volunteered to share their experience as participants in the Childless by Choice Project. However, I suspect that any readers who've ever toyed with the idea of not having children will see their own motives and complex feelings reflected in my participants' responses.

In addition to my deliberate information gathering, my journey included diversionary trips to Philadelphia for a No Kidding! convention, to Maryland to participate in a hang-gliding event with one of the No Kidding! social clubs, and to a "free coffee in exchange for advice" event in Calgary, Alberta, where we invited parents and the public to help a couple with their decision about whether to have kids.

Had I been a desk-bound academic or a scientist with a prestigious grant, I might never have taken the opportunity to experience these events or have been offered the privilege of meeting childfree couples in their homes and in pursuit of their pleasures.

The childless by choice are everywhere: They are your teachers, your neighbors, your colleagues, your sons, and your daughters. Although the majority of the people I interviewed one-on-one were Caucasian, people of very diverse backgrounds are represented in the survey.

THE INTENTION

This book was not conceptualized to be the definitive work on the childless by choice. The childfree by choice have yet to be counted in North America—there are no lobbyists working on our behalf, no powerful political organization, no talking points. Trying to identify the childfree by choice as some sort of homogenous group, based on who we are and what we value, is a bit like nailing Jell-O to a wall. If I leave you with as many questions as answers, trust me, that's intentional.

For many of you, this book will be your first exploration of voluntary childlessness. You may be a parent, a student, a teacher, or childfree yourself. Regardless of who you are or how you came to be reading this book, our common ground is curiosity. We have questions, and these questions open avenues for exploration, and exploration leads to discovery. For the Childless by Choice Project, my agenda was exploration; discovery was the destination. Conclusions, if there can be any, will be left to you.

Two Is Enough is written from the perspective of a small but growing minority of the North American population. I, like most of the people I have interviewed, have no agenda to convert anyone to a childfree life. Nor do I offer my story and others' stories as a cautionary tale, meant to dissuade anyone from considering a life without kids.

When I say "a life without kids," I mean a life without a parental or guardianship responsibility for children. Dr. Carolyn Ray uses the term "ward-free," which can be a useful synonym for "childless by choice" or "childfree," given that some of the childfree are actually not free of children at all. Quite a few of the childless by choice welcome children into their lives by being mentors, teachers, volunteers, advocates, stepparents to grown children, or aunts or uncles. Some admit to needing a regular "kid fix," while others try to avoid children as much as possible.

The voluntarily childless population is a diverse group, and it's for this reason that I use the terms "childfree," "childfree by choice," "childless by choice," and "voluntarily or intentionally childless" interchangeably. "Childfree" is currently the *nom du jour*. However, our pronatalist society does not always know how to interpret this term, and there is the risk that "childfree" could imply motives that may not apply to all who have adopted it as a way to communicate their well-being. (See "Childless or Childfree?" on page 18 for my perspective on this.)

I do not endorse one term over another, because my intention is not to encourage a political or social movement, or to define the childfree in North America. My intention is simply to tell a story that is rarely told, to give voice to those who are rarely heard. It's my hope that this book finds its way into the hands of those people who want and need these stories, and for whom this information is timely or instructive. My hope is that in moving beyond the assumption of parenthood, this book might serve as a compass and a guide for those navigating in a world that has yet to construct pathways for all of us who remain childless by choice, or by circumstance.

CHAPTER 1

Who Are the Childless by Choice?

Miss Vickers was one of my favorite teachers at Lakeport High School. In a school on the southern shore of Lake Ontario known more for its drugs and athletics than for its academics, Miss Vickers stood out. She looked like a nun without the habit—birdlike and intense, but always smiling. She was my English teacher, a grammar Nazi who was determined to prepare us all for a college education, even though she knew that many of us would end up at the A&P supermarket or the General Motors plant instead.

I liked Miss Vickers because she liked us; she was one of a handful of teachers who would volunteer to stay after school and help with the drama club and other extracurricular activities. I have a photo of her playing a villain in one of the student productions. Since she clearly enjoyed working with us kids, I often wondered why she didn't have any of her own.

Until I started the Childless by Choice Project, I had no idea how many people like Miss Vickers were out there. As it turns out, there are a lot. In 2002, a whopping 44 percent of women between the ages of fifteen and forty-four were childless in the United States; in the forty-to-forty-four age group, 18 percent remained childless.[1] Same thing in Canada: 18 percent of forty-to-forty-four-year-olds remained childless in 2001.[2]   .

Back in high school, it didn't matter to me if Miss Vickers was childless by choice or by circumstance. The result was the same—a life without biological children. In the absence of any openly childfree role models, she showed me that it was possible to be childless and happy. That revelation was timely, too, as the idea of a childfree life was something I was just beginning to entertain.

Back in the '70s, in St. Catharines, Ontario, a predominantly working-class city historically populated with immigrants and their kids, a single, childless, thirtysomething woman was pretty rare. If there were any childfree by choice people in my neighborhood, they blended in seamlessly with the rest of the childless folks. No one ever spoke about someone's actively opting not to have a child.

So who are the childless by choice? Are they really any different from the rest of the population? Sociologist Dr. Kristin Park, in an analysis of her own and previous studies, found that in comparison with the general population, the voluntarily childless are "more educated, more likely to have been employed in professional and managerial occupations, more likely to have both spouses earning relatively high incomes, more likely to live in urban areas, less religious, less traditional in gender role orientations, and less conventional."[3]

After years of working on the Childless by Choice Project, I have found this to be mostly true, with the exception of "more likely to have both spouses earning relatively high incomes." Although I did not seek income-range data as part of my survey, plenty of the couples I interviewed had different income levels, and many earned what is best described as a living wage.

Park's findings that the voluntarily childless are more likely to be "more educated" and "less religious, less traditional in gender role orientations, and less conventional" were also true in my findings. It makes sense. After all, people who are more religious, more conventional, and more likely to gravitate toward traditional gender roles are probably also more likely to adopt traditional family models.

The conventional family model of Mom, Dad, and two-plus kids is the default in populations with little exposure to other viable models, exposure that might come from travel, education (formal or informal), or the introduction of nontraditional role models or new and appealing ideas and ideals. In 1998, U.S. census reports showed that 30 percent of childless couples were college graduates, compared with 17 percent of couples who had children. Consistently, researchers find that the more education a woman has, the greater the probability that she will not have children.

In 2002, it seemed every North American media outlet was quoting Sylvia Ann Hewlett, mother of five and author of *Creating a Life: Professional Women and the Quest for Children.* Hewlett had surveyed 1,658 high-achieving women and found that about 40 percent were still childless at age forty-five. According to Hewlett, a "crisis of childlessness" exists among the professional ranks of American women.

Creating a Life sounded alarm bells. The message: Don't delay—have a kid now, or you'll be sorry! The resulting media spin made it sound as if a life without children was not a life worth living.

Hewlett's book focused primarily on childless females who wanted children but had postponed childbearing because of career demands or lack of opportunity. But those women represented only one slice of the childless pie. In fact, 14 percent of the high-achieving women Hewlett surveyed had determined *by the time they were in college* that they would remain childless by choice.[4] These women were the classic voluntarily childfree "early articulators." Yet none of these happily child-free women were profiled in the book.

At the same time that the press was reviewing *Creating a Life,* I was beginning my own literature review. I found out that there are in fact four categories for the childless, ways in which people come to remain childless through their choice, actions, or intent:

1. "Early articulators" are those who make the decision to remain childless early in their lives.
2. "Postponers" are those who delayed having a family and remain childless.
3. "Acquiescers" are those who make the decision to remain childless primarily because their partner wants to be childfree.
4. "Undecided" are those who are still in the decision-making process.

Many of the women featured in Hewlett's book would fall under the category of postponers, but within that category, Hewlett's subjects were limited to women who expressed some regret about the choices they had made—or didn't make.

What Hewlett's work exposed, though, was not just these women's feelings of regret around childlessness, but their regret around the lack of options available to them, options limited by the harsh realities of biology, economics, workplace policies, time, money, and the availability of suitable partners. And though these challenges are universal, the women featured in Hewlett's book were, by and large, middle- to upper-class working women, women who are better off than most North American women, many of whom do not have the luxury to choose from what Duke University fertility expert Dr. S. Philip Morgan calls "competing opportunities": fulfilling, full-time work or other pursuits that might be as appealing as or more so than full-time child rearing. What Hewlett's work did was propagate the assumption that childlessness leads to regret, asserting that those high-achieving women who feel compelled to forgo motherhood amounted to a "crisis of childlessness."

In contrast, the women I interviewed who identified as childless by choice expressed very few regrets. Only 41 percent of them strongly identified with the statement "My lifestyle/career is incompatible with parenthood" (indicated by a 4 or 5 rating on a scale of 0–5). Compare that with the 75 percent of women I surveyed who were strongly motivated to remain childfree because they "have no desire to have a child, no maternal/paternal instinct."

Clearly, this is a different slice of pie than the one Hewlett wrote about. When a person has no desire to have a child, the choice to remain childless seems natural and true to oneself—some would even say it's a no-brainer. Seventy-nine percent of the men and women who identified as early articulators in my survey strongly identified with the statement "I have no desire to have a child, no maternal/paternal instinct." Yet the majority of the people I interviewed recounted a decision-making process that required a considerable amount of thought, time, discussion, or introspection, often made more problematic by the fact that their families and their communities expected them to have children. Then there were those who considered themselves "hardwired" not to have kids and couldn't imagine another way of being.

Among the childfree by choice are people in our population whom society does not expect to have kids: singles, gays and lesbians, and infertile couples. Childfree by choice is as much a way of thinking as it is a way of being. Early in this project, I met a happily childless lesbian who complained about the intense pressure she and her partner faced from peers who thought they should have kids. She reminded me that same-sex couples and the unmarried are making this choice, too.

Because of their diverse natures and sensibilities, the child-free resist stereotypes. In general, I agree with Park's character-ization of the childfree as more likely to be college-educated, less religious, and less tradition bound in their gender roles. Beyond that, I don't know that I can make any other general-izations about the childless by choice in North America, based on my survey and interviews.

CHILDLESS OR CHILDFREE?

What do we call people who don't have kids? Are they child-less or childfree? It depends. Let's take a moment to clarify the nomenclature pertaining to childlessness.

Those who prefer to identify themselves as childfree point out—rightly—that the word "childless" implies an absence, a void, or "less-ness." "Childfree" seems to them like a more positive term, and it makes the distinction between the child-less by circumstance and the childless by choice.

The difference between the two is mostly self-definition. If you are without children because you made that choice, then you might consider yourself childfree or childfree by choice. If you are without a child because of circumstance, rather than choice, you might describe yourself more accurately as childless.

I say "might" because I have had the pleasure of meeting couples who wanted children, struggled through infertility, and came to describe themselves as childfree. I also know people who are happily without children and prefer to describe them-selves as childless by choice—including me. The reason I have chosen to describe myself as such is that "childfree" can imply judgment: that what you are free of is bad for you, based on our common usage of the terms "sugar-free" or "smoke-free." Most of us remove the hyphen from "child-free" in an attempt to neutralize that association. It's a useful trick when writing about the childfree, but it's useless in conversation.

I think we need to acknowledge that in a pronatalist society, "childfree" can be a loaded term. It can imply more than we intend, inviting people to ascribe motives—such as dislike of children—that may not apply to people who are using the term as a way to communicate their well-being. "Childfree" also implies a type of lifestyle that may not accurately reflect the lives of some of the childless by choice I have interviewed: teachers, childcare workers, and those who choose to welcome other people's kids into their lives.

"Childfree" is likely the most politically correct term in common usage at the time of this printing; however, it has yet to be widely adopted by those who are without children by choice. For this reason, I will refrain from endorsing any one specific term and invite you instead to choose the one you feel most comfortable using.

HOW MANY OF US ARE THERE?

We have yet to accurately quantify the voluntarily childless in North America, because the majority of our studies and surveys do not distinguish between the childless by choice and the childless by circumstance; or if they do, they narrowly define the childless by choice as those who have voiced their intent to remain childless in their teens or early adulthood. This ignores the fact that many of the intentionally childless are individuals who may once have anticipated parenthood, but who later made the decision to remain childfree in their thirties and forties—whether because they postponed conception or because of their choice of lifestyle, or a number of other factors.

The limited definitions of the childless by choice used in most studies make it difficult to get an accurate count. Many studies are conducted under the assumption that men and women will decide whether or not to have kids during the time of high fertility. But increasingly we are not doing that, because we are postponing parenthood. In 1970, the average age at which American women gave birth was twenty-one.[5] Now, on average, an American woman gives birth to her first child at age twenty-five, a Canadian woman at age twenty-nine.[6]

Some surveys have also presumed that eighteen- to twenty-four-year-olds can accurately predict how many children they will have. But often they do not. As Dr. Morgan told me during an interview at Duke University, "In the contemporary United States, people have slightly fewer children than they say they intend [to] at a relatively young age. The normative answer is two," said Dr. Morgan. "It's going to be one boy and one girl—that's how people picture their future, so that's the very common answer for that group of people."[7]

However, our circumstances and perceptions change over time. As I have heard in interviews, a woman who perceives her childlessness as undesirable at twenty-eight years old might celebrate her "childfreedom" ten years later. It's tough to count the childless by choice in North America because they are a constantly shifting demographic. We do know that in the United States, the number of women who describe themselves as voluntarily childless increased from 2.4 percent in 1982 to 6.6 percent in 1995 (the most recent figure, according to the National Center for Health Statistics). In Canada, a 2001 Statistics Canada survey revealed that 7 percent of women and 8 percent of men from ages twenty to thirty-four intend to stay childless.[8]

THE CHANGING FACE OF THE CHILDLESS BY CHOICE

Will the childless by choice population continue to grow? Ask a young adult you know. In the United States, childlessness among women aged forty to forty-four has doubled, from 10 percent in 1976 to 20 percent in 2006. Whether this trend will continue remains to be seen. Gen Xers and Yers are the wild cards because they're facing a whole new array of choices, particularly where the definition of family is concerned. Will it be two parent, single parent, same sex, unmarried, blended, or childfree?

The bulk of today's eighteen- to twenty-five-year-old single nonparents, today's generation of emerging adults, have yet to seriously contemplate marriage or having kids. Many of them are still in school, dependent on their parents for financial assistance, or still living in the family home. Parenthood may not be on their radar, and even if it is, their ideas may change as they grow into full-blown adults.

A 2004 *Time* magazine poll found that only 61 percent of Americans aged eighteen to twenty-nine described themselves as "an adult"; 22 percent believing that "moving out of a parent's home" makes you an adult, and another 22 percent felt that "having your first child" does.[9]

Yet this demographic is challenging the assumption that children are an essential component of marriage (and by that measure, I would dare to say adulthood as well). Of those aged twenty to twenty-nine, only 20 percent agreed that the main purpose of marriage is having children.[10]

For those young couples who do opt to have children, they will, on average, have fewer kids than their parents and grandparents. The reasons for this decline vary from increased education and workforce participation to more effective birth control, higher divorce rates, economic uncertainty, and the fact that women are increasingly postponing marriage and childbirth.

The current generation of young women is more likely than any previous generation to delay marriage and child rearing beyond age twenty-five. Most experts agree that peak fertility in women is between the ages of eighteen and twenty-five, so these women are delaying marriage beyond their most fertile ages. In contrast, their mothers, on average, were married by their twenty-second birthday.

Almost all demographers see a direct relationship between postponement of marriage and parenthood and declining birthrates, but continue to debate whether this is a temporary phenomenon or a trend toward long-term sub-replacement fertility.[11] In my interview with Dr. Morgan, he acknowledged that the "fertility window is shrinking" and total births often fall short of intentions, and attributes this fact to postponement and other factors. All demographers agree that the trend to postpone parenthood shrinks the fertility window for women, increasing the likelihood that they will have fewer children than they may have intended or expected previously.

Financial considerations are also a factor. In *Time* magazine's poll of young adults, 66 percent of college graduates surveyed were more than $10,000 in debt when they graduated. Canadians typically don't have as much school debt, but they still feel pressure to delay marriage and kids due to financial instability, which is attributed to debt and a more competitive job market.

"Postponement is the major story in contemporary fertility," according to Dr. Morgan. "Sometimes postponement leads to unanticipated childlessness—not by choice. The alternative is that, as you postpone childbearing, something fills the gap; there are experiences that a person has during those years when they don't have children that can compete with childbearing—that is, they can develop careers or leisure interests that they see childbearing would compete with. And that, for them, raises the cost of having children, and may tip the balance in favor of either continual postponement or not having children at all."

Dr. Morgan reiterated what I had heard from my postponer couples and singles: During the time when we remain childless, paid and volunteer work, responsibilities, and leisure interests "fill the gap" to the extent that there is no discernable void. We also tend to do things sequentially, based on priority, necessity, or tradition: We go to school, we get a job, we find a partner, and we have kids. Or not. We do these things anticipating a reward or some value—a paycheck, a sense of accomplishment or well-being, happiness or security. In today's world, we are increasingly making our choices from a menu of competing opportunities—and responsibilities.

THE FREEDOM OF CHOICE

I don't know what Miss Vickers's menu looked like, but I suspect, given her single status, her past-her-prime-fertility age, and the time in which she lived, her choices might have been more limited than mine. I did have the means and the opportunity to have children. I was married at age twenty-six, during a time when working mothers were common. When Miss Vickers was teaching in the 1970s, intentional single moms were rare and certainly not encouraged or supported, so even if she wanted children, I doubt she would have gone that route. Instead she had us, her students, at least one of whom is extremely grateful she provided a role model for something different.

Had Miss Vickers married, she may still have remained childless by choice or by circumstance, free to go beyond the call of duty and spend extra hours with her students; free to create a family of affinity, rather than blood; free to be the self-sustaining, happily employed person she appeared to be, outside of our traditional idea of family.

A 2000 Current Population Survey indicated that thirty million married couples in the United States do not have children. That total includes empty-nesters along with childless couples, but it represents a growing demographic: couples who are currently living a childfree life. By 2010, the U.S. Census Bureau predicts that married couples with children will account for only 20 percent of households.

The conventional family is a declining demographic. Marriage itself has become optional for many of us. The intentional single parent is now welcome at most sperm banks and adoption agencies. Single-parent families are the fastest-growing segment of our population. Same-sex families who can now choose to adopt or conceive though donors and surrogates are on the rise, too.

So why is it that when we think of families, we still think of Mom and Dad and the 2.5 kids? Because it remains our cultural ideal. And we cling to it like a baby does to his blankie.

CHAPTER 2

The Dawning of Choice

In 1996, I participated in a golf tournament in Roanoke, Virginia. I was in my mid-thirties and just learning the game, so I was paired with a more skillful player, an elderly woman I'd never met. As we waited for the group ahead of us to move down the fairway, she asked if I had children. When I informed her that I was childless by choice, she remarked, "Back when I was having my kids, we didn't have a choice."

Her comment struck a nerve. It was true; my grandmother did not have the freedom of choice I have, and talking with this woman made me realize just how new reproductive choice is for women.

My generation of women was the first to grow up with easy access to birth control pills. I am among the 27 percent of college-educated women, born between 1960 and 1964, who will never have children—not because I delayed parenthood or struggled with infertility, but because I skipped it altogether.

For the majority of married women who came before me, skipping motherhood was not an option. Often the only way they could choose to remain childless was to abstain from sex in a marriage or to remain unmarried. "What a lot of people forget is that childlessness was not an option for so much of human history," Elaine Tyler May, historian and author, pointed out during my interview with her. "Your choice was celibacy or children."[1]

Intentional spinsterhood was exceptional, although history does provide a few notable examples: Susan B. Anthony died childless and unmarried after working tirelessly for civil rights for blacks and women; Florence Nightingale rebuffed numerous marriage proposals in order to pursue her dream of being a nurse and educator; artist Mary Cassatt, famous for her impressionist paintings of mothers and children, remained childless and unmarried.

As Elaine Tyler May noted in her book *Barren in the Promised Land: Childless Americans and the Pursuit of Happiness,* remaining single may have been the preferred option for certain educated women of independent means:

> *"The writer Louisa May Alcott spoke for those 'busy, useful, independent spinsters' like herself who chose to be single, 'for liberty is a better husband than love to many of us.'"*[2]

However, for married women, motherhood remained practically inevitable. Early methods of birth control were unreliable. The most common involved ingesting herbs or toxic potions, using homemade suppositories and douches, or coitus interruptus—commonly referred to as the withdrawal method—which required the cooperation of a very disciplined man.

Not only were these early methods risky, they were also speculative, because most people didn't completely understand the fertilization process. It wasn't until the 1930s that researchers began to understand the effect of hormones on ovulation.

The science of contraception has always failed to keep up with the demand for new methods of preventing unwanted pregnancies. Even if there had been more and earlier methods, our predecessors wouldn't have been inclined to remain childless. Why? Because to do so would have exposed them to stigmatization, financial and emotional insecurity, social isolation, and even religious sanctions.

If you were born before the 1930s and remained childless, you likely would have been marginalized as a spinster, barren, unproductive, unwomanly—distrusted, pitied, or scorned. Throughout the ages, childless women risked divorce, poverty, exclusion, indentured servitude, and even being murdered or burned at the stake by those who equated childlessness with sin or godlessness.

High stakes, right? And for what? The question for the childless woman was: If she were not occupied as a mother, what exactly would she do? Options varied depending on the place and time, but typically it was a very short list: schoolteacher, nurse, caregiver, servant, seamstress, shopkeeper, entertainer, artist, writer, prostitute.

There were few positive role models for childless women prior to the mid-twentieth century. Two of the most famous, pilot Amelia Earhart and actress Katharine Hepburn, lived what many considered "masculine" lives, tinged with tragedy: Earhart, piloting her plane, failed to make an around-the-world trip and was presumably lost at sea, and Hepburn's long-term love affair with the married actor Spencer Tracy, and some suspected dalliances with women friends, led to nowhere but the gossip columns.

Throughout our history, motherhood has been the default in a world that has not offered many desirable alternatives.

TENDING THE VICTORY GARDEN

In the late 1940s and '50s, however, everything changed. Rosie the Riveter, the patriotic icon of American women during World War II, flexed her biceps and expanded the way women in the United States envisioned their roles outside of those of mother and homemaker. Now it was acceptable—no, patriotic—to roll up their sleeves and do a man's job.

That is, until the men came back from the war. Then it was back to the weed-choked victory garden, back to the kitchen and the bedroom, for Rosie.

"Plant more in '44!" was one of the slogans for the victory-garden campaign, but in retrospect, I wonder if there was a subliminal dual message there. In *Barren in the Promised Land,* May points to more overt campaigns aimed at increasing birthrates and attributes much of the resulting baby boom to patriotism:

> *"The passion for parenthood began during the war. The bearing and raising of children became a national obsession with powerful patriotic overtones. Fighting the Nazis with their famous racism and eugenics policies made it unsavory to talk about having children as a duty to the 'race,' so the rhetoric shifted to child rearing as a contribution to the nation. Wartime propaganda continually reminded men that they were fighting for home and family and urged women to turn their postwar energies to marriage and child rearing."[3]*

The propaganda proved effective, resulting in a dramatic rise in U.S. births in 1946 and 1947 that would grow to over four million births each year from 1955 to 1964. Canada experienced a similar increase in births in 1946, which was sustained until 1960, when the number gradually declined.

Although many women gave up their wartime jobs to returning soldiers and returned to their places as mothers and wives, there was no way to turn back the clock. The realization that women could contribute to the common good and find fulfillment outside of the home and marriage bed powered the second wave of feminism. Inspired by the efforts of former first lady Eleanor Roosevelt, the appointed chairwoman of President Kennedy's Presidential Commission on the Status of Women, and Betty Friedan, author of the 1963 book *The Feminine Mystique* and cofounder of the National Organization for Women, women again answered the patriotic call—the call for women's rights and freedom.

Friedan, alarmed by the dissatisfaction her peers in the 1942 Smith College graduating class voiced in questionnaires they completed, wrote *The Feminine Mystique* in part to warn women of the dangers of identifying only with the roles of wife and mother.[4] Friedan was trained as a psychologist, but in the early '60s she remained at home, as a suburban wife and mother who wrote for women's magazines. In the preface of *The Feminist Mystique,* Friedan wrote, "I came to realize that something is very wrong with the way American women are trying to live their lives today."

While Friedan was busy writing what would become the call to arms for a new crop of feminists, the FDA was testing a new drug. Only then, in the early '60s, when the Searle drug company received FDA approval for a new birth control pill called Enovid, would women have both the means and the liberty to pursue a life outside of motherhood.

The effect was swift. North American social scientists took note as total fertility rates dropped dramatically and intentional childlessness became one in an expanding menu of newly sanctioned choices. Childfree women were heralded as trailblazers at a time when expanding roles for women made the stay-at-home mom seem positively quaint, and women began to turn their attention to the world outside.

STOP THE BREEDING!

Declines in North American births in the 1960s were fueled, in part, by the apex of world population growth, which topped out at an annual rate of 2.1 percent between 1965 and 1970.[5] As a child, I wasn't aware of the alarming statistics, but I understood the threat of overpopulation. It had something to do with my peas, which I had to eat because there were millions of starving children in Africa. There wasn't enough good, nutritious food to feed all the people on Earth, so we should be grateful for what we had.

On Human Rights Day in 1967, the United Nations issued the World Leaders Declaration on Population, which included the statement:

> *"[T]he population problem must be recognized as a principal element in long-range national planning if national governments are to achieve their economic goals and fulfill the aspirations of their people."[6]*

Environmental activists, warning of a population explosion that would threaten Mother Earth, pleaded "no more" to earth mothers. Intentional childlessness became the politically correct choice for progressives and activists as zero population growth became a cause célèbre.

Reacting to the threat of overpopulation, leaders around the world enthusiastically endorsed contraception and sterilization. In the late '70s, India's government offered financial incentives to men who underwent vasectomies. Deng Xiaoping, a prominent twentieth-century Chinese politician and reformer concerned that overpopulation would lead to economic hardship for China, created a one-child policy that was often unevenly and brutally enforced by local birth planning commissioners, who felt their political future was tied to meeting their quotas. The implementation was roundly criticized as cruel and draconian, but it was necessary, some argued, to protect both the economy and the ecosystem.

Necessary—and effective. From 1960 to 2005, China's total fertility birthrate fell from 5.9 to 1.7 births per woman, and India's fell from 5.8 to 2.8.[7]

North America's response to the threat of overpopulation was much more low key. During the 1960s, government and public agencies looked for ways to educate parents on family planning, or to advocate responsible parenthood. By 1970, the birth control pill was widely available, and family planning education was being publicly funded in both the United States and Canada, even while there were still laws in place banning contraception. In 1965, the U.S. Supreme Court overturned state laws that prevented married couples from using contraceptives; in 1972, the court extended the right to contraception to unmarried persons.[8] Canada decriminalized contraception in 1969.[9]

In 1966, both Canada and the United States had a total fertility rate of 2.7 births per woman, which meant that on average, each woman would have borne two to three children in her lifetime. By 2005, Canada's rate had steadily declined to 1.5 births per woman, while the total fertility rate in the United States fell to 1.8 in the late '70s and then began rising slowly, back to the current (as of 2009) rate of just over 2.

Unlike in China or India, financial incentives or policies mandating family planning proved unnecessary in North America, as access to contraceptives and expanding opportunities for women became the primary forces driving lower birthrates. Not only were jobs opening up to women, but women themselves were opening up to the reality that they could look beyond marriage and motherhood for identity and fulfillment. The unattached and independent woman, the career girl about town, the feminist, and the sexual revolutionary became iconic role models for modern young women and gave them the breathing room to explore other dimensions of womanhood.

THAT (NEW) GIRL

My Barbie never had a Ken. She was a hip single girl who designed her own clothes, had her own apartment, worked a variety of cool jobs, and knew how to flag a cab. She was Ann Marie.

Played by Marlo Thomas in the late-'60s TV show *That Girl,* Ann Marie was a struggling actress who comically juggled a series of temp jobs in Manhattan. She had a boyfriend but managed to delay their engagement until episode 113. And kids weren't even on her radar. Pressed into service as an emergency baby sitter for a neighbor, she was grateful when the father of the baby finally came to relieve her. In the shower, sudsing up before an audition, she sang, "Rock-a-bye baby in the treetop, boy am I glad you're home with your pop!"

Ann Marie was the chaste TV version of the "Cosmo Girl," an ideal marketed and epitomized by *Cosmopolitan* magazine editor-in-chief Helen Gurley Brown, author of *Sex and the Single Girl,* in which she famously proclaimed, "Good girls go to heaven, bad girls go everywhere."

By the 1970s, the sexual revolution, feminism, and youth counterculture flavored much of the social and political lives of North Americans. In the best-selling 1971 book *The Baby Trap,* the beautiful, doe-eyed advice columnist Ellen Peck warned her readers against becoming "genetic narcissists" sucked in by corporate America's "babysell." She cautioned that in the pursuit of advertising dollars, "the media have built up a 'motherhood' mystique that verges on the hysterical." Voluntarily childless herself, Peck advised her readers to "stay free. At least consider the option of childlessness." The idea that women and men were better off without children was controversial, but she clearly understood the timeliness of her words: "For the first time in history, the option is easily yours to take."[10]

The voluntarily childless came under the close scrutiny of social scientists in the late '70s and '80s, who hypothesized that voluntary childlessness was a trend, rather than an aberration. In the '80s, sociologists Veevers and Houseknecht revealed motives and rationales for intentional childlessness that pointed to a desire for greater freedom and self-determination.

Veevers surveyed 156 voluntarily childless persons (including thirty-six men) from southern Ontario, Canada, and found that the common perception was that parenthood would limit or compromise other, more desirable life options. Houseknecht's research reviewed twenty-nine previous studies of the voluntarily childless and noted that both men and women agreed on the most frequently cited motives for remaining childfree: freedom from the responsibility of child rearing and freedom to be spontaneous and to pursue activities they believed offered a greater opportunity for self-fulfillment.[11]

Much of this perceived opportunity for self-fulfillment was coming from a workplace culture increasingly open to women. The long-running '70s hit *The Mary Tyler Moore Show* opened with Mary Richards, a thirtyish, single, childless news producer, gleefully flinging her beret in the air. Even though the real Mary Tyler Moore was married, had a son from a previous marriage, and was the coproducer of her own show, women across North America idealized Mary Richards's life and began to suspect that their dream careers might be incompatible with motherhood.

WOMB? WHAT WOMB?

Toronto, 1981. I'm being interviewed for my first real job in the fashion industry. I am wearing a navy blue wool suit, navy pantyhose, navy pumps, a navy and white pin-striped blouse, and a bow tie I've fashioned out of a silk scarf. I once padded my bra, but the padding I wear now is designed for points north, shaped to square my narrow, round shoulders.

Fashion, always a telling barometer of the feminine mind-set, had signaled the arrival of the career woman. Peasant blouses and ponchos made way for pumps and pantsuits, the jackets structured and padded so that women could stand shoulder to shoulder with their male coworkers. In the 1980s, pin-striped androgens replaced earth-mother hippies while feminists, failing to rally enough votes to ratify the Equal Rights Amendment, urged their sisters to challenge sexual discrimination in the workplace. The corporate office became the staging area for the right to work and financial independence. Economics came into play as the two-income family became the norm, and socially and economically empowered women endeavored to live their American dream.

Early-'90s prosperity, optimism, and efforts to assimilate women into our corporate culture spawned an emerging demographic: DINKs (double income, no kids). For the first time, childlessness was associated with a middle-class lifestyle funded by discretionary dollars and women's freedom to focus on career, marriage, and hobbies.

For many, this lifestyle was short lived. The majority of women in North America did not want to forgo motherhood entirely. Inspired by media role models like Katie Couric and Martha Stewart, who appeared to combine career and motherhood successfully, women followed suit, FedExing breast milk home when they went on the road and maintaining schedules so tight that five hours of sleep was considered a luxury.

Some women managed the lifestyle effectively, while others found the Supermom existence unattainable or as fragile as a Fabergé egg. In my interview with Barbara Risman, a sociologist and former cochair of the Council of Contemporary Families, she called the Supermom ideal a "myth that was born in the 1980s as women moved into the labor force." This version of the working mom involved a scenario in which women "would seamlessly be able to be the same moms and provide all the same kind of support, love, and care . . . they always have and work an eight- or ten-hour day on top of that—they would carry a briefcase in one hand and a baby in the other, and it would all be easy to do."

However, women began to discover that they "just couldn't do this," said Risman. "The way our workplaces had been constructed—to expect a worker to leave the home at eight o'clock in the morning and get back home at six at night, fifty weeks a year—presumed that worker had an unpaid domestic partner to do everything else that it takes to live a life, from having clean underwear to taking care of babies to taking care of elderly parents who needed to be taken to the doctor in the middle of the day. We had constructed a world of work presuming every worker had a wife, and these women didn't have wives."

As Risman pointed out, women with higher incomes could "buy out" quality takeout food, daycare, and cleaning services. "Yet there still is a lot of stress because kids, particularly young ones, take a lot of time; even beyond what you can buy out, there is a great deal of feeling as if you're never doing anything well enough."

Millions of women who felt the need to choose between their work and motherhood followed the example of advertising executive J.C. Wyatt, played by Diane Keaton in the 1987 Hollywood hit *Baby Boom,* who, after inheriting a baby, loses her coveted career and ends up happily domesticated, making baby food in Vermont. In the words of J.C.'s boss, Fritz, the story message is "You can't have it all."

The switch from career track to mommy track created what U.S. demographers refer to as the "baby boomlet," or the "baby boom echo." This new wave of babies, born between 1977 and 2008 to the original demographic of baby boomers, rivaled the postwar boom in terms of sheer numbers. In 2007, at the predicted apex of the U.S. boomlet, 4.3 million babies were born, matching the previous record of 4.3 million births recorded in 1957.[12]

BABIES, BABIES, EVERYWHERE!

I was twenty-nine when my husband and I moved from Canada to the United States, in 1990. In our new home state of Virginia, we received the gracious Southern welcome-wagon reception. Our new neighbors offered pies, country club sponsorships, restaurant recommendations, and gardening advice—all accompanied by plenty of questions: "What church will you raise your children in?" "Are you thinking private or public schools?" "Have you found an ob-gyn yet?"

I found these questions odd not only because of how personal they were, but also because they presumed we had children, or at least were planning for them. We were not. Our new acquaintances, however, hadn't considered this possibility. It seemed everyone in our little pocket of suburbia was a parent. It took some time, but I eventually did find an outlying contingent of women who had responded differently to the "you can't have it all" message and were choosing childlessness. These women had rejected the notion that they could juggle the demands of their career, or their calling, with the responsibilities of motherhood. They stayed on the job track, convinced that if they took off time to have a baby, their hard-won careers would be jeopardized.

After all, if a spitfire like Meredith Vieira couldn't pull it off, who could?

The year before my move south, TV journalist Vieira had joined the *60 Minutes* team, and her short tenure served as a cautionary tale to career women everywhere. She had just had her first child, and she'd made a deal with executive producer Don Hewitt to work part-time for two seasons before coming back to work full-time. But before those two years were up, she was pregnant again. The deal was off and she was soon replaced by Lesley Stahl, who had a husband who worked out of their home and functioned as the primary caregiver to their teenage daughter.

The number of American working moms peaked in 1997. The four years following marked the first-ever documented decline in workforce participation by married mothers with infant children, dropping from 59 percent in 1997 to 52 percent in 2004.[13]

Now, over a decade later, the media portrays the Supermom as either an Overstressed Automaton or a Hollywood Mom who outsources the cooking, cleaning, and kid ferrying to prepared-food purveyors, domestic help, and chauffeurs. Today, many women look at these characterizations and are either repelled by or resigned to the fact that they will never be able to maintain their career path and have a family—unless they win the lottery. Many women have come to the conclusion that they must either make a choice or compromise.

Oftentimes, the compromise is economically motivated. Some couples opt for one parent to stay at home with the kids because it doesn't make financial sense for both parents to work. So, though we do hear about Mr. Moms, the someone who's most likely to stay at home in an economy in which childcare costs often equal or exceed take-home pay is the actual mom.

Mr. Mom was a movie, not a movement. Stay-at-home dads are equally capable caregivers, but they remain a small minority. According to the U.S. Census Bureau, there were just over 140,000 stay-at-home dads in 2006.[14]

Women have come to realize that the Supermom model is an impossible dream without increased help from their husbands or partners—and many of them have simply given up and embraced the reality. The hope that a couple will coparent and keep the division of labor somewhere around 60–40 or, better yet, 50–50 is an unrealized ideal for the majority of families. According to Barbara Risman, who did a U.S. study on egalitarian marriages with children, this division of labor is rare.[15]

In an attempt to reclaim the promise of the successful working mom, Stephanie Mencimer proposed the baby boycott in her 2001 article of the same name in the *Washington Monthly*. She warned that women were not having children because of an antiquated and hostile environment that required "women to make impossible trade-offs between work and children." She suggested that we could manage low birthrates and skilled-labor shortages by making our workplaces more family friendly, attracting talented and educated workers who might not otherwise be in the workforce because of family obligations, and by allowing existing workers the job security they need to take maternity/paternity leaves.

Mencimer suggested that women hold out for what they needed to effectively parent and contribute to the workplace; that included part-time work with benefits, subsidized childcare, and a commitment from their husbands to share the domestic duties. "Then—and only then—should women agree to fire up the oven."[16]

The baby boycott has begun to take root in North America, though not as intentionally as Mencimer advocated. In the years since her article was published, little has changed. Women continue to postpone child rearing, waiting for what they need to feel secure and supported as working moms. Others have given up on waiting for affordable daycare, part-time work with benefits, and the husband who can function as a full partner in raising a child. Faced with the threat of the fertility deadline, many women have jumped in and abandoned careers to forge new identities as stay-at-home moms. Others go back to work after maternity leave and come home to a second, domestic-work shift, with or without a dad to help out.

Then there are those who look at this menu of choices and lose their appetite. They leave the table hungry for more satisfying fare, or they come to the realization that they were not craving parenthood in the first place. For many women, this menu might be like a chalkboard, changing daily. Men are in there, too, also confronted with choices and helping to expand the menu as we continually redefine gender roles and what we call family.

CHAPTER 3

Assumption, Decision, or Something in Between?

Bobby and Jenny, sitting in a tree,
k-i-s-s-i-n-g.
First comes love,
then comes marriage,
then comes Jenny and the baby carriage.

When I was five or six, I would sing this little schoolyard ditty to tease my friends about their first crush. A child in the '60s, I imagined that I would marry and have kids someday. My would-be husbands included adorable Tony from my second-grade class and the elusive Geoffrey, whom I dumped in the fifth grade for TV heartthrob David Cassidy (who played Keith Partridge).

My imaginary kids were a boy and a girl, of course. But beyond that, it got fuzzy. Unlike my girlfriends, I hadn't picked out names, nor did I spend any time thinking about what they might look like, or what I would actually do with two kids. As I grew into my teens, my imaginary kids seemed increasingly blurred, out of the picture, in the life I was dreaming up as I considered what it would be like to travel the world, run my own business, or teach.

By age fifteen, I had made up my mind that I wasn't going to have kids, and told my mother so. She didn't appear shocked, but I remember her saying that I might change my mind later in life. As she spoke, I imagined a ticking time bomb set for some random day in my thirty-fifth year, an incendiary mix of hormones and longing that would explode my being and rewire my brain. I didn't want to believe this would happen—that my mind and heart were hostage to something called maternal instinct—but I decided to hedge my bets. I decided I would cram as much of the good stuff of my dreams into my early adulthood, certain the arrival of a child meant a departure from my dream life.

I never felt that same trepidation about marriage—I knew I wanted to marry. While many of my peers were playing the field during the sexual revolution, I was a committed monogamist. I met my husband when I was twenty-two; a mutual friend introduced us after telling my future husband that she had found the woman he was going to marry. The timing was a bit off, as we were both dating other people, but after spending a few hours together those other relationships suddenly seemed wrong. So we gave each other a two-week deadline to break off the current relationships and met again for our first real date in a funky little soufflé restaurant in downtown Toronto. I cannot recall if it was during that date or the following one that I told him I was inclined toward a life without children, but I do remember how relieved I was when he remarked that he had no burning desire to have kids, either.

We married four years later. At that time, I was running my own business, a fashion sales agency, which required overnight travel; my husband, Robert, was about to take on a new job that would require frequent trips overseas. There would be times when we wouldn't see each other for weeks, and the subject of children didn't come up again until we moved to the United States two years later.

I knew from experience that life circumstances influence decision making, which is why I felt it was important to adopt, and further define, the four categories of decision makers for the purposes of the Childless by Choice Project survey, to see if there were any significant differences in motives or process.

I asked my survey respondents to choose the category with which they identified most from the list below:

- Early articulators are those who make the decision early in their lives, generally without influence from a significant other.
- Acquiescers are those who make the decision to remain childless primarily because their partner wanted to be childfree.
- Postponers are those who delayed having a family and ultimately decided they didn't want kids.
- Undecided are those who are still in the decision-making process.

In my sample of 171 participants, 113 self-identified as early articulators, 15 as acquiescers, 37 as postponers, and 6 as undecided. I invited the undecided to participate in the survey because they identified themselves as childless by choice but acknowledged that they may change their minds. I felt strongly that if I wanted to understand the decision-making process, I needed to interview and include those who were currently in that process.

I have come to understand that the undecided identity is largely an indication of age or stage in the process of choosing to parent or not to parent. Some of those who described themselves as postponers or acquiescers would likely have also identified themselves as undecided had I found them earlier in their decision making. Again, this is the problem we encounter when we look at the childfree life simply as a choice, rather

than a process. It's both, really. It's a series of choices, or decisions made over a timeline in which life experiences, observations, and people act as influencers.

Most of us, parents and nonparents alike, start with the assumption of parenthood and then, over time, either assimilate
or adopt the assumption because it feels right, or are motivated
to challenge it because it doesn't.

CHALLENGING THE ASSUMPTIONS

According to the National Marriage Project's report "The State
of Our Unions: 2003," nearly 70 percent of Americans disagreed with the statement that "the main purpose of marriage
is having children." Yet for the majority of couples, the idea
that you get married and have kids remains firmly entrenched.
Aunties pinch your cheeks on your wedding day and ask how
long it will be before the children start coming. Friends lobby
for baby buddies. Parents counsel you to wait until you're financially stable to have kids, yet blanch when they discover
that the car you just bought is a two-door. The question is not
"are you planning to have children?" It's "when are you having
children?"

This assumption of parenthood persists even while the assumption of marriage has lost its power in modern courtship.
Marriage or partnership is no longer a prerequisite for parenthood. One of the fastest-growing segments of the North American population is the single-parent household—and that's not
due entirely to a high divorce rate. Much has changed in the last
half century, and what we define as "family" has changed, too.

International adoption, in vitro fertilization, surrogates,
baby daddies, and sperm and egg donors have made marriage
optional and single parenthood intentional. Many same-sex
couples, denied the right to marry in most states, aspire to be
parents as well. Where there is a will, there is often a way.

The same will exists for those of us who feel no desire or inclination to have kids. However, common assumptions often work against us: Our peers and our parents are certain that we will change our minds, or that children will come whether we plan for them or not, and that we will be better for it.

One notion, reinforced by Hollywood's childless characters, is that the life we have chosen is unnatural, even a bit sinister or heartless, and that the introduction of a child into the orbit of a childfree person will melt away years of resolve or knowing, making us whole and happy again. Who has *not* seen *A Christmas Carol* or *Baby Boom*? These movies work to propagate stereotypes about the childfree, suggesting that a life without children is infantile, unfulfilled, or tragic, and reflect the underlying beliefs, ideals, and expectations of the majority population.

Lodged in our cultural permafrost are the carcasses of three ancient mammoths: (1) the expectation that we will all become parents one day, and it will be a rewarding experience; (2) the idea that parenthood is a critical stage in human development and maturity; and (3) the belief that all couples should be encouraged to parent, regardless of their ability or desire.

We will examine these mammoths more closely below and in Chapter 7. However, you don't have to be a scientist to recognize that these beasts are at risk of exposure in this new climate of change.

The optimism of youth and the assumption of parenthood are reflected in Canadian statistics, which show that only 7–8 percent of young adults do not plan to have children, compared with the much greater percentage of people who find themselves childless in their forties by choice or by circumstance. What happens in those fifteen to twenty years in between?

Infertility, lack of opportunity, delay, divorce, disability, lifestyle, sexual orientation, indecision, and intention come to mind. Many people intend to have children, but somewhere along the way their desire is thwarted or they change their mind. They may find themselves without a partner when the time is right. They may encounter circumstances beyond their control that make parenthood problematic, if not impossible. Or they may postpone parenthood and eventually conclude, "Our life is good just the way it is."

DECONSTRUCTING THE DECISION MAKING

The childless by choice show up on the timeline at the point when parenthood moves from being an assumption to being a decision. For an early articulator, this could happen at age eighteen; for a postponer, it could be at thirty-five. When you begin to challenge the assumptions around parenthood, when you begin to see some value in remaining childless indefinitely—a fate some of your peers can't even begin to imagine—you find yourself on new ground. Parenthood becomes an option, not something that is fated, inevitable, imperative, or integral to your well-being. You are free to exercise choice.

When I began to interview couples, I noted that they appeared to be operating under a different set of assumptions than the three "mammoths" I outlined earlier. Their decision making arose out of a very different framework of beliefs or ideals.

First, they did not have the expectation that we will all be parents one day, or that parenting will be a rewarding experience. While some acknowledged that the experience of parenting a child was rewarding for most of the couples they knew, very few of the couples I interviewed presumed that parenthood is rewarding for all. Despite the barrage of endorsements from gushing new moms and dads, they could not ignore the fact that some parents appeared unhappy or disappointed, having not gained the rewards they had expected from parenting. Thus, my interviewees retained some skepticism.

For many of the childless by choice, a life without kids is not only imaginable but also rife with possibilities for self-actualization. Rather than regarding parenthood as a critical stage in their development and a sign of their maturity, many of the people I interviewed imagined another path by which they would grow and evolve as human beings. Early articulators were particularly adept at this, as they had great difficulty imagining the parenthood path for themselves, even when they were children, and had therefore invested more time and energy in living, and planning for, a life without children.

Not one childless by choice person I interviewed believed that all couples should be encouraged to parent, regardless of their ability or desire. In fact, some admitted they would be terrible parents; they had spent time imagining themselves as parents or imagining how a child might feel being raised by people like them, and decided they did not want to be a party to that outcome. Others felt, after a period of self-analysis, that the only way to be true to themselves was to question the societal assumption that they would be parents, based on their sense that they lacked the necessary inclination, desire, or instinct that would have made child rearing a natural expression of who they are.

SOMETHING IN BETWEEN

In between the assumption of parenthood and the decision not to be a parent are the undecided, as well as some of the self-described early articulators, and people who intended to become parents but for one reason or another never had the chance to do so. "Choice" may be a difficult word for these people to use when it comes to describing their decision-making process. Sometimes it looks like the chalkboard menu at the café near closing time: Two entrées have been rubbed out and you're allergic to the third, which means you're left with the challenge of finding happiness in something you wouldn't otherwise have chosen for yourself. But the self-described childless, childless by choice, and childfree have shown me it is possible to embrace the leftover choices and find happiness in the in-between.

Like Amber, who struggled with fertility treatments until she decided to remain childfree. Like Claudia, who might have had kids if her first husband, an alcoholic, had been a more suitable candidate for parenthood. Like the early-articulator women I interviewed who told me that without the desire to have kids, they felt they had no choice but to remain childfree. All these women self-identify as childfree by choice because they acknowledge that they made choices that led to a child-free life, and they take full responsibility for those choices.

About halfway into this project, I adopted the mantra "happiness is a choice." I don't know why this particular saying stuck in my mind, but it did—and it served me well during times when things weren't going my way. I recall thinking that so many of the people I was meeting through this project seemed to have adopted this mantra, too.

TWO COUPLES, THREE TYPES OF DECISION MAKERS

One of the reasons I asked my respondents to identify themselves by decision-making category was so I could compare their processes and their rationales. I was fortunate to find Neil and Julie and John and Kathy, two couples in their mid- to late thirties who had met through their eastern Virginia No Kidding! chapter and had become close friends. Julie identified as an early articulator, Neil as an acquiescer, and John and Kathy as postponers. I was delighted when they agreed to be interviewed as a group, as this allowed me to gather representatives of three of the four decision-making categories in one room to compare and contrast.

The interview was scheduled for a Saturday evening at John and Kathy's house, and I had made arrangements for my videographer, Robert Smith, to videotape the interview. When we got there, the two couples were playing poker in a newly decorated game-and-media room. The decor was distinctly nautical, reflecting John's career in the Coast Guard, and featured a wall-mounted flat-screen TV, comfy media loungers, a game table, and a wet bar.

John, thirty-four, was the youngest of the group; his wife, Kathy, was thirty-seven; Julie and her husband, Neil, were both thirty-eight. As we set up the video equipment, Julie admitted to being nervous. As I explained my goals for the project, it naturally came out that both Robert and I were childfree, and I noticed that the group seemed visibly relieved. They said they had known other childfree folks who had been portrayed unfairly in news segments, and my interviewees had been afraid that they would end up being misrepresented as well.

I directed my first series of questions at John and Kathy, the self-described postponers, starting with whether they'd expected to have children when they were in their early twenties.

"I think it was an assumption," John responded. "It was something that was going to happen eventually . . . when the time was right."

Kathy had had a much different experience. She claimed that until she was in her late twenties, parenthood never entered her mind. "I was never one of those girls in junior high who was naming my twins. I just never, ever gave it a thought. Which isn't to say I was for or against it; it never crossed my mind. And so I guess I was leaning toward being childfree then. Kids were never part of my equation at all."

Kathy, the firstborn in her family, always had trouble imagining herself on the conventional path. "First of all," she said, "I couldn't picture myself married . . . ever. I could just never look that far into the future."

Julie, the early articulator, spoke up: "I never thought I was going to have kids. And when my parents would ask me about it, I would say, 'Ask me in ten more years.' Ten years would pass, and it was the same thing. I'm just not feeling that maternal pull and was never interested at all, even though I had a great time with my nieces and nephews."

Unlike Kathy, Julie did think about marriage: "Oh yeah—I never wanted to be alone. I like sharing my life with someone."

Julie's husband, Neil, the acquiescer, recalled the time before he and Julie were married: "I guess I'm more like Kathy. I never really gave having kids any thought. I was young, single, and having fun. I guess I just figured I'd make my decision about it in ten years, when I was married."

John also wasn't thinking about his future children, even after he married Kathy, although he held it out as a possibility. "We set a deadline for ourselves: our early thirties, because we didn't want to have children later in life and be older parents. So we set a date and reached that date—"

"And we set another date," Kathy interjected.

"And then another date, and another date," John added, laughing. "Then we took a look at ourselves and said, 'Wait a second. What's going on here? There's a bigger picture here.' So we examined it and decided that kids just weren't in the cards for us. We liked the way our lifestyle was progressing at that point. So that's when we made the final decision, in our early thirties, to remain childfree."

Kathy offered up some precautionary words at this point: "John and I totally did the one thing that people should never do when they get married: We never talked about kids. Obviously, that showed us something. We never talked about pros or cons until we got to our deadline. One day John would be for having kids, because of the potential regret; I would be against it. Then, three days later, it completely flip-flopped. We did a ton of debating and discussing. It's not something we came to, at least for ourselves, overnight."

"It was very fortunate," John recalled. "As she said, we didn't speak about having children before we got married, which I do not recommend; it should be discussed. But we didn't discuss it, and luckily, we ended up on the same page. We were very fortunate."

At this point, Neil stepped in to talk about how different his experience was, from the acquiescer's perspective. "We did have the conversation before we got married," he said. "I knew through more casual conversations that we'd had in the past that she didn't want kids. But before we actually got married we did sit down, and she said, 'I don't want to have kids. So if you're ever going to want to have them, this is going to be a problem.' I think that if I had married someone who really wanted to have kids, I probably could have been talked into it. But I was sort of glad Julie didn't want them. So, yeah, it was something that was understood before we got married."

ONCE THE CHOICE HAS BEEN MADE

I asked Neil if at any point he'd feared that he might ultimately regret his decision to enter into a childfree marriage. "Not for me, there wasn't. I think a lot of family members and friends still probably think that we're going to regret it. But I know that I'm not going to." Neil went on to say he felt very comfortable with his decision—then and now. He recognized, however, that Julie bore most of the burden of the stigma and the external pressures.

Julie smiled in acknowledgment: "Yeah, because I come from a Catholic family. You know, you're expected to have kids: 'What's wrong with you that you don't want to have kids? Who's going to take care of you when you get older?

Why don't you have kids? You've got to have kids!' Now my parents are much older, and they're kind of coming to terms and saying, 'You know what? You're fine, because you can't count on your kids to take care of you when you're older.' And they kind of realize that whatever your choice is, it's your choice. But it's taken them a long time."

Neil came from a much smaller family—he has only one sibling—so his exposure to family pressure was limited. "I wouldn't call it pressure. I think my sister would really like for me to have kids. And my parents have passed away, so there's no pressure there. But other than that, I think everybody pretty much always knew that I didn't really want them."

For Julie and Neil, a lot of pressure to procreate came from coworkers. "We're both teachers, so every day at school you get it," Julie said. "'When are you and Neil going to have kids?' people ask. We used to work together in the same school, so they know both of us. I always just said, 'We're not having kids.'"

However, it didn't end there. Julie recalled incidents of not-so-subtle lobbying: "'What's wrong, what do you mean? You know, you're not too old. It's okay.' The assumption is, when you grow up, you get married and have children. That's what everybody does. We really are seen as different from people who do have kids—very different. And you do a lot of explaining."

John was also raised Catholic but suspected his siblings and their progeny saved him from the kind of grief Julie had experienced: "Fortunately for me, I have three older siblings," he said. "I am the youngest of four, and they all have children. So my parents got their fill of grandchildren. By the time I came along, there was no pressure. Kathy is a different story, though."

"I think my pressure is more internalized," Kathy admitted. "It's just me and my brother, who isn't even married, so my parents have no grandchildren. They have no prospects of grandchildren. They're living in Florida, where everybody flips out pictures of their grandkids like they're playing cards. So I've had a hard time."

Kathy felt sorry for her parents, she said, "because I really felt like I was letting them down and denying them something that they needed. When I finally went ahead and said, 'Look, this is the deal: We're not having kids,' I think their reaction was something like 'Yeah, we kind of figured that out.' And I was like, *Well, what does that mean! Don't you think I'll be a good mother! I'll show you!"* Kathy laughed as she recalled her own reaction. "Again," she said, "they realized it probably before I did. I was the one with more of an issue. Mom would say, 'I ran into so-and-so, and I saw pictures of her grandkids.' Gee, thanks. So now she shows pictures of our dog."

As Kathy talked, I recalled my own mother's adoption of my brother's dog as a kind of surrogate grandchild prior to the birth of her only grandson. I felt compelled to ask Kathy, "Does the dog get presents at Christmas?"

Kathy laughed and pointed to a cluster of dog toys. "You can see the pile. She's the granddog, and the only granddog, so my mom gets presents for her birthday and Christmas. The good thing with both sides of our family is now they're both remarkably accepting of our choice. In fact, my mom, if people ask her, has a statement: 'John and Kathy are practicing zero population growth.' She says, 'That way, it shuts them up.'"

ARTICULATING THE MOTIVES

The conversation turned to the couples' reasons for remaining childless, and how they deal with people who want to know why they don't have kids. When the question comes up, Neil is cocked and ready: "I just say, 'Hey, I teach high school—that's the best birth control there is.' That's my standard answer, so I don't have to get into too much more detail than that."

Kathy's approach has to do with her having been a high school teacher, too. "I tell people, 'I have seen the future, and it's just not pretty.' They should make every person who wants to have children spend a week in a high school as an observer, because it's just amazing. Parents have no idea what goes on."

To Julie, who currently teaches middle school, I said, "I imagine when you get home, you just want to decompress."

Julie gushed, "Oh, yes! It's a wonderful thing coming home to a quiet house and a couple of cats, and peace and quiet. That's the only way you can live, is how I feel. We have eight nieces and nephews between us, from ages eight to twenty-six. There you go! That's all the gifts and kid stuff I need."

I asked Julie, "What was your biggest motivation for remaining childfree?"

"I like my life how it is. I didn't feel a void. I didn't feel like I needed more out of my life." Over the years, Julie has retained this sense of well-being: "I am very happy with how it's been and how it's going. I just don't see the need to change it. I really don't. I am very fulfilled. This is it for me. This is wonderful."

"I kind of agree with Julie as far as liking the freedom," Neil added. But he acknowledged that his motives were different: "I don't know that I had a motivating factor to not have kids, to be honest. I just don't think I've ever really found a motivating factor to *have* kids. Like Julie said, I've never felt the need."

When I directed the question to John and Kathy, John concurred, "Neil took the words right out of my mouth. I would just add that in addition to not having a motivation to have kids, the financial aspect played a big part as well. When you start crunching the numbers and looking at what it takes to raise a child, put him through college and all that, you're thinking, *Gee whiz! I could retire when I'm fifty, if not earlier, if I were to forgo those expenses."*

Kathy described experiencing a series of motives, which changed as she matured. "There are so many. It's kind of shifted throughout the years. My biggest issue, though, was that of the people I know who had kids, the majority of them don't seem fulfilled to me. They don't seem happy. They're always talking about when they have grandkids, as if they're willing to blow past the next twenty years so they can get to that point where they have grandkids, so they can have the fun without any of the responsibility. Whereas John and I feel that our life is perfect the way it is. Why would I want to change it?"

I asked Kathy if she ever imagined how it might be to be a parent. She said that she had, and that she thought she and John would have been great parents, but that it wouldn't have been a natural progression for her.

"It has nothing to do with our lack of ability to parent. Because I do think our upbringing and backgrounds are similar. When I was trying to foresee the future with my Magic 8 Ball, I didn't ever see myself as a parent. I talk to people who are close to me, like my mom or my brother, and they'll say the same thing: 'We never pictured you with kids.' It's just not something that comes naturally to me. I'm around a baby now, and I'm the awkward one. 'Oh my God, it's crying. What do I do?' I was born without that maternal gene."

INSTINCT OR CONDITIONING?

As soon as Kathy mentioned the "maternal gene," I jumped to my standard follow-up question: "Do you think there is such a thing?"

"I do," Kathy said. "I think certain people are born with that instinct. That's what they want to do; they played with baby dolls, and they are brought up to want children. I think that's just a natural phenomenon. I don't think I have that, and I'm okay with that."

I turned to the others: "A paternal instinct—is there such a thing?"

"Not for me, there isn't." said John, shaking his head. "I've never experienced a paternal instinct."

"I know people who definitely have the maternal instinct," Neil said. "I mean, we've known couples who have gotten married, I think, so they could get to the having-children part. And we've known couples who have had children to make their own relationship better. But we know several people who definitely have the instinct. That was the only thing they talked about until they had the child."

"I'm very comfortable around kids—my nieces and nephews, and my friends' kids," Julie said. "I've got that maternal bond with those kids, but just for that day or that period of time—then I'm done. And that's all I need."

"I relate to older kids," said Neil. "I just don't relate to the little toddlers."

Julie laughed. "When Neil's sister had two girls, we would go over to baby-sit and he would have to leave. He just could not handle them. I would say, 'Fine, just go home.' Because I had nieces and nephews already, it came very naturally to me. It didn't mean that I wanted to have my own, though, you know? But he's not comfortable with little kids at all."

I asked the group, "So why do you think people have kids?"

Julie jumped in: "Because they're supposed to. You're supposed to have them."

Kathy hesitated. "I have to be tactful. I think most people have kids because they don't think there's a choice; it's the next step. When you get married, you have a child. It's just the natural progression. And I think the majority of people who have kids don't put a lot of effort into discussing it—whether it's right for them. I just think they go right down that road."

Neil thought some people have kids "because there's something missing in their relationship, and they think having a child, or children, is going to make it better. From what we've seen, it usually doesn't. It just makes it worse because you have kids and you're more stressed out, you're not getting as much sleep as you were, and there are financial problems. There're all kinds of added pressures that a lot of people don't think of until they actually have the child. All they're thinking of is coaching Little League and teaching them to throw a baseball. They're thinking of all the fun times, taking their first steps and all that. They don't think about all the really miserable times, too, and the problems that can come up."

"They're cute when they're six months old, just out of a bath and smelling like baby powder," said Kathy. "They're not so cute when they're thirteen and in juvenile detention. I think people look at the bright side of it, and they don't tend to weigh the negatives."

I wondered aloud, "So, when we weigh the pros and cons, do we look to our family and friends to see what they've experienced?"

In his and Julie's case, Neil didn't think so. "I think both of us pretty much knew that it wasn't going to happen."

Julie explained, "My very best friend has three kids—and that's great. But she knows I'm not going to change and she's not going to change. It was just such a natural thing to not have kids."

"But the media portrays it differently," said Kathy. "You have all of these Hollywood celebrities on this baby boom. Everyone is having kids. Everything is just wonderful; everyone should do it."

John was the only one who said he really did look to his family to identify the possible pros and cons of parenthood, and he noted a marked difference in the quality of the spousal relationship when he compared his relationship with Kathy with the relationships of couples who did have kids: "I shall leave some individuals nameless to protect the innocent," he started playfully. "We have relatives who . . . not that we've asked them, but we've observed them. I can tell you that our relationship is infinitely stronger than some others' that are close to us."

ASSESSING THE PROS AND CONS

Kathy picked up where John left off—on the subject of relationships. "Well, you know, people fight about certain things," said Kathy. "One of the major things people fight about is children. When you eliminate those factors, it becomes that much easier." She talked about the luxury of time and attention. "John and I spend a lot of time together. We're able to talk to each other as adults about what's going on in the world and various things, as opposed to worrying about what Junior might be doing.

"I see parents who, when they speak to each other, don't really talk—they simply discuss the children. We've eliminated that, so we're able to have conversations. I think that helps us a lot as a couple. We're able to focus on each other a little more, instead of putting it off until the kids get out of the house."

Neil talked about his special relationship with Julie. "I think we were pretty much meant to be together. We've finished each other's sentences since the first week we met. But I honestly think that if we had children, that would probably be the end of us. No offense, honey," he laughs, "but we have very different ideas as far as child rearing goes. I mean, the main thing we still argue about and joke about at the same time is that she swears that no child of hers would ever attend a public school. She thinks that with a private school, you get a better education and you're more prepared for the future. My idea is public school is the real world and that every child should have to experience that. Because once you get out of school, there is no sheltering. You have to be able to deal with the real world."

"So even without kids, you argue about kids," Julie said. "It's a good thing we don't have kids!"

Both couples had identified the potential cons by envisioning themselves in the parent role and imagining how different their relationship would be if they did have kids. I wanted to reframe the question to invite them to identify what they had actually experienced as a benefit of a life without kids, so I asked, "What's the best thing about being childfree?"

Neil identified one of most frequently articulated benefits: "That freedom to do the things we want to do, with nothing holding us back. We love to travel. When school gets out in June, we can just pack up and go. To me, that's very fulfilling."

"The best part of being childfree?" John picked up. "As Neil said, the freedom. We don't have to look for that baby sitter. It's very liberating. We enjoy that lifestyle."

"How about the downsides?" I asked, wanting to see who among the group had evaluated the potential risks of remaining childless.

John admitted that earlier in his processing of things, he had considered the risk of regret, but he wasn't feeling any of that yet. "I think time will tell, but I'm very optimistic that we made the right decision."

Julie could think of only one downside. "The difficult thing is meeting people around your age who don't have kids, who are available or want to do the same things you want to do. You really are quite often left on the outside of things. It's Mother's Day, or at work you have all the moms talking about their kids and what they're doing. But that's a minimal problem. I wouldn't trade it."

Julie had taken full responsibility for her decision, so she was reluctant to complain. She said, "The choice has been made, you know?"

I was interested to know how these couples navigated their unconventional pathway. I knew from my own experience that a life without children comes with its own set of challenges, like that age-old question of who's going to take care of you when you get old. So I posed the question to them using that adage, particularly since it had come up in previous conversation.

Neil responded with a rhetorical question of his own: "Why have a child just so you can burden them thirty years from now, when you're too old to take care of yourself?"

Julie agreed. "You cannot count on that. You can have a child. You can raise your child. But when your child grows up to be an adult, they're going to be their own person. That's really unfair to put that on them."

"That's the ultimate selfish act," said Kathy, making a face. "They talk about childless people being selfish. Still, I find that I get asked that question a lot. Depending on who's asking, I have various answers. Usually, I try to argue that elder care is typically not provided by the child. When it's someone being snippy, I usually say, 'With all of the money I'm going to save by not having children, I'm going to hire a hot Swedish guy named Sven to wipe my wrinkly old butt when I'm old.'" She laughs. "Because most people are going to end up in some sort of retirement home or nursing home. Even people who have kids—and that's a tough gamble to make, to gamble your life, your happiness, on the assumption that someone is going to be there to take care of you when you're old. I'm not willing to take that gamble. I figure John and I will go out in a blaze of glory!"

At that point, Julie extended an offer, born out of affinity and friendship: "We'll take care of you! Call us up."

FINAL WORDS

As we wrapped up the interview, I asked the group if they had anything else they wanted to add.

Julie took the opportunity to challenge a common stereotype: "Being childfree does not mean we don't like children; it means we don't care to have children of our own. We just want people to accept that: It's okay to be different, and not everyone has to have kids to be fulfilled. I do know some people get so much joy out of their kids. I see it in my friends who have kids. And I don't envy that, because I feel like I have so much joy in my own life. I appreciate theirs, and more power to them, but we have our own. This is our way of having joy."

Neil cautioned against the influences of others: "I would just say to make sure that the decision that you're making is for yourselves and not because your parents want grandchildren, or because your friends are pressuring you."

"I'd just stress that it is a *choice* to be made," said John, reflecting on his process as a postponer. "It's not some predetermined, predestined type of event in your life. It is your choice to make."

Kathy hoped her involvement in this project would help others like her. "I think the biggest thing I'd want people to get from this is that they're not alone, and that there are many people out there that have made this decision. When John and I were making our decision, I didn't know that. I thought there was something wrong with us, and I really felt isolated because I couldn't find enough information and books or materials on this lifestyle and people who have made this choice. So I think it's important for people to know that they're not alone."

A WORD FROM THE UNDECIDED

Much of what I have come to know about this decision-making process came from the undecided couples I was privileged to meet on this journey. Tara and Patrick and Harpreet and Manmeet were two of the couples who shared their experiences with me. I found Tara when I came across a paper online that she had authored. In it, she explored the childfree rationale and defended her own decision to remain childless by choice. I met

Harpreet at a film-outreach conference in Washington, where we chatted briefly about the challenges of being childless in a culture that doesn't know how to respond, beyond pitying us.

TARA AND PATRICK:
THE CHALLENGES OF INDECISION

When I contacted Tara to request an interview, she informed me that she was reconsidering her decision to remain childfree, and that she and her husband, Patrick, were still undecided. I recognized that interviewing this couple presented a wonderful opportunity to see just how a decision is made, in real time.

Tara was conflicted. After years of being happily childfree, she was beginning to experience pangs of longing for a child, particularly when she saw a mother with a cute baby. However, she was concerned that she might be romanticizing the idea of motherhood and ignoring the reality. At the time of our first interview, Tara was twenty-seven and Patrick thirty-one. They had been together for eight years and married for over five. Their indecision was a tremendous challenge for them as a couple, particularly since they were the type of people who believe in the power behind intention.

I asked if they'd had a kid conversation before they were married.

"Yes, definitely before we were married," Tara responded emphatically. "Because it's pretty important that you have a kid conversation before you commit to someone *for life*."

"I think it was more 'I'm not ready for kids—yet,'" Patrick recalls. "And then, finally, 'Are we really going to have kids? Maybe not.'"

Tara concurred that kids had not been on her radar. "I wasn't expecting, at nineteen, to meet the man I was going to spend the rest of my life with. It was surprising for me. I had always said, 'I don't see myself with kids. I don't see that happening for me. Maybe when I'm older.' I endlessly had this five-year plan: *In five years, I'll think about having a kid.* And then that five years continues to move up a year. I think I'm at year eight of a five-year plan.

"At a certain point, we had decided we weren't going to have kids at all," Tara continued. "I guess it was about a year ago when we started going, 'Well, maybe—maybe we should think about that; maybe that is something we want.'"

Patrick smiled. "I think it was a year ago when *you* decided."

Patrick explained that lately, Tara was leaning toward having kids and he was still unsure. He suspected that her maternal instinct had begun to kick in. Tara reminded Patrick that she didn't believe in maternal instinct. She confessed she often felt awkward around children, and that Patrick seemed much more at ease around children than she did.

We talked about how Tara's friends and family had reacted when she and Patrick declared themselves childless by choice. "My mom was kind of hopeful that I would change my mind," said Tara. "She would say things like 'Well, when you're done with your education, we'll talk about it again.' There was a lot of resistance, people saying, 'Oh, you wouldn't want a baby? But they're so cute. Imagine a mini Patrick and Tara.' Then there are the people who've just recently had kids, and they say things like 'Oh, it's awesome, it's the greatest gift. You're really missing out.' They love their kids, and they should. They go through these gushing phases: 'See, you should have kids, too. Join this club.'"

Tara and Patrick are only children. They told me that if they did decide to become parents, they would choose to have only one child; they had previously agreed that it would be one or none.

"That's the biggest thing," acknowledged Patrick. "You kind of feel bad for your mom." He also understood that Tara felt the bulk of the pressure regarding this particular guilt. "She really wants a grandchild," Tara explained. "She's tried to make do with the dogs—we have two pugs. But at a certain point, it became 'Okay, that's enough, I want the actual child.'"

I asked them, "What happens if Tara wakes up and says, 'I want a kid,' and Patrick wakes up and says, 'I don't want a kid'?"

"That happens a lot, actually," Patrick admitted. "Quite often Tara will be the one to initiate that conversation. Then I'll be like, 'Whoa, wait a second, didn't we just decide that we're not going to have a kid?' Usually I just leave it alone until she switches back. Usually that's the way it works."

Tara acknowledged that she felt bad for Patrick. Her indecision was a point of contention. "There's only so much you can put your partner through," she said. "Patrick responds by saying, 'Why don't you take some time? In three months, let me know where you're at.' Some of my friends now ask me, 'Are you on the kid thing this week, or off?' It's become a joke. I'm in real turmoil about it, I guess. 'Turmoil' is maybe too dramatic a word—it's not *that* painful."

I could tell by her body language, though, that "turmoil" was a pretty accurate description of what she was feeling, so I asked Tara, "What's the hardest thing about making this decision?"

"It's a long-term decision. People talk about the kind of pressure you have when you buy a house or a car, or when you make a career choice. That's nothing. Those are so changeable, so fluid."

"If you decide you want a child, you're going to have to change your lifestyle," said Patrick. "It may not be better, it may not be worse, but it's definitely different."

"It is," Tara agreed, "and it's different forever."

For Tara, the pressure to have a child came from family, friends, and her own periodic longing. Patrick was ambivalent. He enjoyed spending time with kids, but he wasn't sure he wanted to make the changes to his life that being the father in an egalitarian marriage required. The fact is, he had already fathered a child when he was in his teens, though his son had been adopted by his ex-girlfriend's husband and the family was living in another country. I couldn't help but wonder if this was the reason he appeared to give Tara the lead role in their decision-making process.

A year and a half after our first interview, Tara emailed me to tell me she was pregnant. They had decided to stop taking birth control and let nature take its course. They had soon become pregnant, but then lost the baby and went through a period of deciding whether they wanted to try again. They did, and when Tara emailed me, she was approaching the second trimester of what would be a full-term pregnancy.

I had already planned to go back to Canada and do a follow-up interview with them, and I arrived at their door two months before the birth of their baby boy. They were decorating the nursery and making plans, paving the way for Baby. Tara was scouting future playdate candidates in the neighborhood, and Patrick was planning a work schedule that would allow him to work from home and coparent with Tara. It was obvious to me that this couple was ready and willing to embrace parenthood—with intention, commitment, and enthusiasm. I left their house that day thinking that they were bringing one lucky little boy into the world.

HARPREET AND MANMEET:
MANAGING CULTURAL PRESSURE

Harpreet always thought she would be a mom. Her husband, Manmeet, is the eldest son in an Indian family and in his early twenties he had his eye on what he hoped would be his future wife. Manmeet had noticed Harpreet, the pretty Sunday school volunteer, at the Gurduara (their place of worship) and arranged for a mutual friend to introduce them; they married within a year. When I met them they had been married for over eight years yet remained childless by choice.

At the time of our first interview, Harpreet and Manmeet were twenty-eight and thirty-one years old, respectively. Both were very involved in the Sikh community, collaborating in efforts to promote Sikh culture and their Indian history through film and music. This commitment took them to cities all over North America, and to India for weeks at a time.

Our interview took place at Harpreet's parents' home, as the couple were between houses in anticipation of a cross-country move. I asked them to recall their first conversation about kids. "We talked about kids even before our marriage," Harpreet remembered. They made plans, they imagined the kids they would have: "We love kids. We taught at camps. We wanted to be teachers."

Manmeet recalls their hectic lifestyle at the time: "For the first three years of our marriage, we thought that maybe we should have a stable relationship before we had kids, and we hit the pause button for a while."

Harpreet interjected to clarify: "I had just graduated from high school when we met, and I said, 'Let's just finish college.' I took credits like crazy, and I finished in three years. At that point, Manmeet was working and had a decent income coming in. Financially, we could have kids, but I didn't want to risk my career. I said, 'Let me look for a job. Let's be like normal couples—get a job and then have kids.'"

Harpreet's career path in media meant long hours and travel. Now an award-winning documentary filmmaker, she regularly travels across North America screening her films. Manmeet is her partner in this endeavor, functioning as crew and coproducer when they go to India to shoot their films on human-rights issues. But even when they return to their home in America, they cannot escape a pronatalist Indian culture.

"We were the first to get married in our family," said Harpreet, explaining that in their cultural tradition, Manmeet, as the firstborn son, was expected to have kids—and soon. "Everyone kept saying, 'Why aren't you having kids? Why aren't you having kids?' It was driving me crazy. I was sick of it."

Harpreet describes how this cultural pressure, intended to encourage them to have kids, had the opposite effect. "I was like, 'You know what? I'm not going to have them. I'm going to do what I want to do.'"

Manmeet describes a series of conflicting priorities: "We always play these hypothetical games: *Oh, if we had kids, they would do this.* Harpreet wants our kids to be skating in the Olympics, and I want them to be musicians. I would want them to do well; I might go to India for a few years to get them trained. So we have all these ideas. It makes it harder. If we had kids, we would have to do all these things, and some of them are not possible now."

Manmeet talked about some of the short-term goals they had set, which included their forthcoming move to Texas so they could get the support they needed to produce their latest film. "I just wish that there were more parents that we knew who said, 'Okay, we were able to do all this; we were able to have kids and everything got done.' Some of the parents we've come across who had their kids early have said, 'We had our kids and now we're done with it.' It was like it was one of those 'to-do' things, one of those tasks in life—the checklist. We just feel that there has to be a more profound reason to have kids."

"Not because everyone's doing it," added Harpreet. "There has to be a reason for it, and we haven't found that reason."

Manmeet contrasted their experience and their process with that of their peers: "I think for most couples it's more spontaneous; there's not much of a thought process that goes into it."

I asked them if anything else had influenced their decision making. Harpreet responded that she felt pressure from her family and community. Indeed, during the interview, her grandmother came into the adjoining kitchen and said something in her native language. Harpreet gave me a rough translation, saying, "My grandmother says we should have a child."

Harpreet continued, "My family says, 'Have kids, you'll have a full life.' For me, right now, the way I define my life as being full is completing the goals I set for myself. I don't want to be forty with kids, looking back and thinking, *I should have done this; I wanted to do this.*"

One of the couple's primary goals includes working with youth in Sikh communities. "We have been very involved with camps, going out and teaching music, having workshops for the kids," explained Manmeet. "I've been doing it for the past twelve years. What we realized is that kids are wonderful to work with. We would like to help more kids through camps or educational programs."

But even that pursuit comes with demands. Women see Harpreet interacting with the children, she said, and they say, "You're so good with kids at camp—have your own." At that moment, Harpreet couldn't imagine how she could do both. "When I'm at camp, I don't have my own child; I'm available to everybody. If I have kids, I don't know if I'll have time for camp, because I'll want to do stuff with my own kids."

So Manmeet and Harpreet continued to remain stubbornly childfree in a prochild culture, enduring pointed questions and the assumption that something was seriously wrong with them—or, more accurately, her.

"Oh, are you infertile?" is the question that Harpreet noted is one of most annoying. "It's always toward the woman," she concluded.

Manmeet agreed with his wife: "It's demeaning. The older generation, they think you're physically incapable of it, and the finger pointing is always toward Harpreet, and it infuriates her."

Harpreet stiffened, and her voice took on a defiant edge. "It's none of their business. They pity me, and that is what bothers me the most. They say they will pray for me. Pray for what? Don't waste your prayer. We're fine, we're happy. But in my community, it's *poor husband, his wife can't have a kid.*"

So while Harpreet felt compelled to rebel when her community pressured her to have the children she didn't feel ready for, Manmeet idealized a life of "parenting the world," valuing the opportunity to impact the lives of hundreds of children, rather than those of the few biological children he might have someday. He and Harpreet both believed it necessary to sequence their life goals—school, marriage, time as a couple, career, and then kids. Yet they felt that something as important as raising children should not be treated as simply one task in a series of checklist items, and that parenting their biological children may not be their divine purpose.

THE LIBERTY OF CHOICE

When parenthood moves from being an assumption to a decision, people are able to experience the liberty—and consequences—of their own choice in the matter rather than settling on the notion that parenthood is a given. These couples valued the process of examining, on a case-by-case basis, the decision to parent; they looked deep into their own hopes and expectations, assessing their desire, skills, and suitability as parents. Most did not buy into the notion that effective parenting is a skill people learn on the job. (Though Tara did say, a year into motherhood, that she thought her son had taught her how to care for him more than any of the parenting books she read had—but she still didn't believe in the idea of maternal instinct.) For many of the childfree, the idea that everyone can and should parent seems naive or risky. What if you failed to be the parent you hoped to be? The risk of being bad or unhappy parents sometimes seems worse than the threat of regret for them.

When Julie said, "The choice has been made," it made me wonder: Is regret around the decision to remain childfree any worse than or different from the regret we might experience about other decisions? Imagine parenthood as one offering on a menu of equally enticing indulgences. You make a choice, and you do so knowing that there's always the risk of wishing you hadn't—many of us have experienced what I call menu envy: *Ooh, that looks good; maybe I should have ordered that.*

During my interviews, I was reminded continually that we risk regret every time we make a decision or fail to act. What many of these couples were doing in the course of their decision making was a form of risk management. They were minimizing the risks in their lives by choosing between the life, or lifestyle, they had come to love and an uncertain future as parents. These couples were not risk-averse; however, they were inclined to assess the odds of succeeding before they made their decision.

If you identify as a free-spirited, spontaneous person and you think doing a risk assessment about parenthood is about as romantic as a prenup, or if you want to leave yourself open to all that comes your way, you will likely resist the notion that parenthood is a decision. "Damn the risks," you might say. "How will I know unless I try? I'm more likely to regret not having children than having them."

About halfway into my first year of interviews, I began to suspect that certain personality types are more predisposed to remaining childfree, which I've detailed further in the next section, "The Personality Theory." If you look at intentional childlessness solely as a process, it's easy to slip into thinking that it is the same for everyone. It is not. The early articulator's road is very different from the postponer's. The pathways are sometimes direct routes and sometimes slow and meandering. The only thing we share is an understanding that for some of us, parenthood is not inevitable, nor should it be. But that's just some of us.

Most people living in North America are, or will become, parents. The decision not to have children remains the exception. Even today, when marriage is increasingly optional, the idea that kids are optional, too, has yet to be entertained by the majority. It exists only for those who can imagine a life without children and think it appealing, a choice that exists only outside of the presumption of parenthood.

THE PERSONALITY THEORY

After combing through the transcripts and the data I collected during the Childless by Choice Project, I devised a theory: that certain personality types are more inclined to remain childless than others.

When I began surveying the childless by choice, about a third of the way into my interviews, I began to see a pattern emerging: Many of my participants were self-described introverts. They used this term as a way to explain their aversion to the noise and hubbub that typically come with young children, or as a way to explain their preference for "quiet" or "peaceful" households that afforded them some "alone time."

"I like being around a lot of people, I'm good at parties, but I'm an introvert in the Myers-Briggs [Type Indicator] sense," said Tamara. "I need to recharge alone, in a quiet place."

Sara said, "If I don't get my alone time, I get really grumpy."

"When I was a kid, I preferred drawing and writing alone in the woods to playing with my siblings," said Misty. "I'm still very much that way today."

Dr. Kristin Park had also found a personality component in her study of the childless by choice: "I heard about things like impatience, or 'I am a really sensitive person, I'm an introverted person, and I don't do well with a lot of activity and noise.' One thing that was interesting was how much people reflected on their personality traits. That was something I hadn't seen much in previous studies."[1]

Quite a few of the people I interviewed admitted to being "planners." They preferred to carefully plan a trip rather than wing it, though these same people valued spontaneity in their day-to-day lives. Jerry Steinberg, founder of No Kidding!, noticed that there were very few smokers or heavy drinkers in the No Kidding! social clubs in the mid-'80s—far less than were typical in the social milieu at the time. He deduced that the childfree are typically inclined to consider the consequences of their actions.

I also noted that my participants tended to approach their decision about whether to have kids very deliberately—logically, rather than emotionally. They did not want to leave it up to fate or whim. I heard the words "accountable," "intentional," and "conscious" used to describe the process.

My participants were, by nature, also inclined to challenge the conventional thinking or ideals around parenthood and nonparenthood. They volunteered to participate in this project in part because they felt it necessary to challenge assumptions and policies they thought were wrong or unfair.

This reluctance to toe the party line seems to have less to do with stubbornness or disrespecting authority and more to do with people naturally asserting themselves, refusing to be the square peg forced into the round hole, because of a strong sense of self.

More than a few of my participants would be described as high achievers and were reluctant to commit to something as huge as parenthood without having at least some confidence in a successful outcome.

My first exposure to perfectionist tendencies as a motive to remain childfree was in Jeanne Safer's book *Beyond Motherhood*. Safer wrote that the childless by choice "reject parenthood, in part, because they lack the requisite 'burning desire' they bring to other major life enterprises. Many see themselves as perfectionists who could never live up to the impossibly high standards they would impose on themselves. They also don't want to risk imposing their unrealistic expectations and exacting standards on a child."[2]

Safer's study and my own support the idea that certain personality types are predisposed to choose a life without children of their own. Had I been aware of this apparent personality component earlier in the process, I might have asked all of my participants about personality traits, or have asked them to take a personality-assessment test. This idea came too late, so I can only hope that my successors will take on this challenge and add more nuance to the sparse literature that exists on this subject.

CHAPTER 4

Eighteen Reasons (and More) Why We Don't Have Kids

At age thirty-nine, I found myself in a birthing room, trying to remember the breathing techniques I'd learned in prenatal class, counting minutes between contractions, and thinking, *I made the right choice. I can't imagine being a mom.*

I was there as a birth coach. The mother-to-be was a young woman I had been mentoring for four years, a college-bound high school senior. Her pregnancy had prompted a slight delay in her plans. Fortunately, the birth of her baby boy turned out to be a blessed and transformational event—for both of us.

I was first introduced to the little guy at the second sonogram, when he revealed his manhood, his hand raised as if waving at us. I was his mom's birth buddy over six weeks of prenatal classes; I had a duffel bag packed and ready, waiting like an expectant father for the phone to ring. When it finally did, I breathed, massaged, and prayed through seven hours of labor that ended in a celebration of the birth of a healthy baby.

Later, as I pressed my face against the nursery window, watching him sleep peacefully in his little blue hat, I scanned every nook and cranny of my heart and mind for any sign of longing. *Do I want this?* I waited for some little voice, or a twinge. There was nothing.

Okay, so . . . why don't I want this?

I didn't know. However, this experience of *not* wanting when so many of my peers *were* wanting planted a seed, a question, that would launch my journey with the Childless by Choice Project four years later. What could possibly motivate someone to forgo the experience of parenthood, the love of a child? As it turns out, the reasons are numerous.

Below are the eighteen motive statements whose creation I describe in the introduction of this book. They are listed in descending order, beginning with the motives that most compelled the participants most to remain childfree or the statements that received the highest ratings, indicating participants' strong identification with them. A sample of the full questionnaire can be found in Appendix B.

MOTIVE STATEMENT 1:
I LOVE OUR LIFE, OUR RELATIONSHIP, AS IT IS, AND HAVING A CHILD WON'T ENHANCE IT.

In the first round of numbers analysis, this motive turned up as the fourth most compelling. But when I took another look at the data analysis for each motive, I realized that this motive statement was poorly worded, as it presumed the respondent was currently in a partnership. That meant that respondents who were currently without a partner had no choice but to give it a rating of zero, even though they may have loved their life as it was or believed that children do not enhance a relationship. When I went back to individual questionnaires, I saw that those respondents who were not in a relationship had done exactly that—given this statement a zero, or "not applicable," rating. I decided I needed to reanalyze the data on this one motive, using only the respondents I knew to be married or in committed partnerships. When I did, this motive was clearly at the top of the most-compelling list. Of the Childless by Choice Project respondents who were partnered, a whopping 85 percent rated this motive statement a 4 or a 5.

Are children the glue in a successful marriage? If so, voluntarily childless couples are not buying it. In my interviews with couples, they all expressed satisfaction with their relationship and with their lives, and some feared children would be detrimental to that satisfaction.

When I interviewed Wayne and his wife, Gina, they confirmed that marital or life satisfaction was a major factor in their decision making. "Neither one of us was really in the frame of mind that we needed something external to be satisfied with our life or our relationship," said Wayne. "I think that self-reliance and being happy with who we are played a big part in shaping us as a couple, and individually."

"I like the status quo," wrote Jodi, in response to my follow-up questions, "and I really can't envision how a child would improve my life." Her husband, Chris, agreed: "We have a happy, loving, fulfilling relationship as we are now. It's reassuring to think that the dynamic of my relationship with my wife won't change."

This was a common theme for the men who, when asked to consider whether they felt that being without children actually enhances a relationship, responded with a resounding "yes!" Michael wrote: "I find way too many couples lose themselves in a child and fall out of love with their partner, never to regain the relationship and love they originally had for one another."

Trond had witnessed this disconnect and had formulated his own theory: "When a couple has a baby, that relationship changes. Like it or not, nature ensures the survival of the child by making the mother now love the child more than anything else, which leaves the father (at least until he gets used to it) playing second fiddle to the mother/child relationship. That's fine if you go into the baby-making experience knowing that, but I think most men find out the hard way. By staying child-free, we are lucky to maintain the relationship that brought us together in the first place."

Studies show that these couples have good reason to feel somewhat apprehensive about bringing a child into the mix. When I started seeing evidence of the marital-satisfaction motive, I recalled a *USA Today* article I'd read back in 1997, titled "Couples in Pre-Kid, No-Kid Marriages Happiest," that cited sociologist Mary Benin's long-term study of spouses and reported that marital satisfaction is greatest before the kids arrive and starts to decline sharply after the birth of the first child, reaching a low point when the kids are in their teens; it doesn't rise again until the kids are grown up and have left home.[1]

In 1979, psychologist Sharon Houseknecht compared voluntarily childless wives with mothers (each group had the same educational, religious, and workforce-participation rates) and found that the childless women experienced greater marital adjustment and satisfaction, which the respondents attributed to more shared activities and conversations with spouses.[2]

Some of the childless by choice couples I interviewed saw risks inherent in child rearing, particularly to their emotional and intimate lives as couples.

In a *New York Times* op-ed published on Valentine's Day in 2005, Judith Warner, author of *Perfect Madness: Motherhood in the Age of Anxiety,* shared the opinion of many of the childless by choice that the roles people adopt when they become parents can be "love killers." She asserted that our current "Supermom and Superdad" model for raising children—in which children's demands repeatedly trump parents' needs as a couple—is crazy-making, and that the only way to avoid that pattern is to nurture the parental relationship until it is solid enough to handle children's assault, and then set strict boundaries.[3]

Some childfree couples I interviewed also had rejected the current model of parenthood, perceiving it as a recipe for disaster. Instead, they idealized the more authoritarian method their own parents had employed, in which kids were not the center of their parents' universe.

It's easy to understand why, in a climate in which 50 percent of marriages end in divorce, a couple might be reluctant to risk a relationship they have come to cherish. The carcasses of our friends' and families' broken homes are like roadkill; a fleeting glimpse of them serves as a cautionary tale. Many people might be asking themselves, *If my friends who eagerly anticipated parenthood can't successfully navigate the journey from couplehood to parenthood, then what are my chances, especially given that I am less motivated to pursue parenthood as a goal?*

MOTIVE STATEMENT 2:
I VALUE FREEDOM AND INDEPENDENCE.

This was the second-most-compelling motive for the group; 82 percent of the women, 78 percent of the men, and 100 percent of the twenty- to twenty-nine-year-old respondents gave it a rating of 4 or 5.

Gina, thirty-four, considered parenthood in terms of the trade-offs: "I feel that if you decide to have kids, you need to sacrifice a lot—primarily your freedom—to raise a child right. I do not wish to sacrifice my freedom. My parents had me without considering this, and I suffered for it." I found myself identifying with Gina—and with her parents' reaction to having a child. Like Gina, I valued my freedom as a childless woman. And I imagined that if I were to have children, I too might have grown resentful in light of feeling constrained by parental pressures and responsibilities.

Nancy, who was also thirty-four when I interviewed her, had never imagined herself in a mom role and, once married, resisted pressure from peers to conform: "I remember receiving this Hallmark card. The outside of the card said, 'You're Married!' The inside asked, 'So, when are you having kids?' My independence and my ability to be flexible in my life are too precious to me. Perhaps if I had a desire to have children, I would be willing to compromise my idea of freedom and independence." For Nancy, though, that desire wasn't there.

Jerry, fifty-nine, loved his teaching job and valued the "freedom to take a job that is extremely enjoyable and rewarding, even if it doesn't pay enough to support a family of four, five, or six."

MOTIVE STATEMENT 3:
I DO NOT WANT TO TAKE ON THE
RESPONSIBILITY OF RAISING A CHILD.

Of the male respondents, 82 percent rated this statement a 4 or 5, compared with 70 percent of women. However, women were able to articulate more specifically why they wanted to be free of this responsibility.

Survey respondent Grace wrote this in response to my follow-up questions: "Well, I don't think it's fun to be a parent a lot of the time. The responsibility must be enormous. There are hazards and failures at every turn. I think the reality of children is so different from people's ideas about child rearing, and the whole thing comes as a shock."

"I've already had the experience of raising my brother," wrote Jodi. "I remember a huge fight when my mom asked my brother about a permission slip for a school trip. He said, 'Oh, I had Jodi sign it, since she takes care of me anyway.' I didn't understand why I was wrong in signing the slip, and that made her even more furious. That was a pivotal point for my mom. She began to see that I was the invisible parent. Later she apologized for putting a lot of responsibility on me at a young age. I think she thought she ruined parenthood for me. I don't believe so. I have really great life skills and I owe that to Mom for giving me responsibility for myself and others."

Another respondent, Tracie, had tasted parenthood and didn't want to go back for seconds: "My first husband had a child from a previous relationship. Up until he was four years old, we would have him over on the weekends and on some holidays. It was fun to play Mom two weekends out of the month and every other Christmas. However, we ultimately obtained full custody and I got to experience firsthand how difficult parenting is. It was all very overwhelming for me at twenty-four, and the marriage eventually failed. The experience of it has never left me, and I think it played a big part in my decision not to have a child."

In his master's thesis study of more than 450 childfree women and men, Vincent Ciaccio observed "a solid understanding of the responsibilities of parenthood. They understand that children will reallocate their time, affect their career ambitions, their finances, their privacy, and their social activities, and they do not want these changes taking place."[4] This was true of the majority of my survey respondents as well; they did have a very realistic understanding of the responsibilities of parenthood, and that knowledge had factored into their decision making. Unfortunately, I did not have the data to determine statistically what type of responsibilities—related to finances, childcare, or household or child stewardship—my participants were reluctant to take on.

MOTIVE STATEMENT 4: I HAVE NO DESIRE TO HAVE A CHILD, NO MATERNAL/PATERNAL INSTINCT.

In hindsight, I realize this statement, too, could have been better worded, as it is in fact two statements: (1) I have no desire to have a child; and (2) I have no maternal/paternal instinct. My efforts to isolate the two in subsequent interviews prompted me to ask what would become one of my favorite follow-up questions: Is there such a thing as a maternal or paternal instinct? I asked this question often, and I got a lot of different answers:

"Absolutely," said Jennifer. "I've seen it in my friends and have felt the lack of it in myself."

"Absolutely not!" Theresa responded emphatically. "I don't have it. None of my childfree friends have it. There are far too many children who are neglected, abused, and not wanted for me to believe in such a thing."

Elaine agreed with Theresa on that point: "I believe it's sociocultural brainwashing. If maternal behavior were instinctual instead of learned, even those of us who didn't like or want children would be having them."

Many of my participants did believe that there is such a thing as a maternal or paternal instinct, but 75 percent of the women and 64 percent of the men I surveyed felt strongly that they were the exception: They did not have the "instinct" or the "desire" to be parents.

"I have the wisdom to raise a child, but not the desire," wrote Sue. Or the maternal instinct, as it turned out: "It's just absent. Kids don't interest me much until they are about ten. My sister is the same way, and she didn't have children, either."

Tracie could recall only "a few brief periods where I felt like I wanted to become a parent. However, they passed, and when I look back on these times I now realize that those feelings were mostly driven not by the desire to be a parent, but by something going on in my life that I was not happy with, such as my relationship or my job, and having a baby was a sure way to change those situations—for better or for worse."

Some of my participants acknowledged feeling maternal toward nonrelatives and animals, even while admitting they had no desire for biological offspring. Grace, age fifty, wrote,

"Now that I'm older, I'm quite maternal toward kids in their late teens, twenties, and thirties. Recently a young man I know who has trouble with his own parents leaned over to me on Mother's Day with damp eyes and whispered, 'Thank you for being the mother I never had.' That was quite an honor!"

Misty made a distinction between human and animal babies: "Although I do not like babies, I do have a maternal feeling for baby animals. I am caring for a sick baby guinea pig right now. I never played with dolls as a child—only stuffed animals. My siblings all want kids, and one has two already, so it wasn't the environment. Am I just wired differently, maybe?"

Wayne works at an animal hospital and said, "I care for a lot of animals. Whatever paternal instincts I might have, I project into different areas. Not that it takes the place of having kids, but whatever energies might be focused on raising kids may be diverted to other goals."

Bill didn't want to repeat the mistakes his parents and their peers had made by having a child without first thinking about it because it was expected of them. When he read Ellen Peck's book *The Baby Trap,* he became convinced he should remain childfree, because he felt certain he would be another "uninterested and unmotivated father."

Bill was not alone among the men I surveyed. The reason I included "paternal instinct" in this statement was that many of the men I'd encountered during my research phase acknowledged that they had no desire to have children and thought it was unfair to bring a child into the world without the benefit of an enthusiastic and committed father. These men felt that if you do have a child, you should be prepared to share the burden of raising that child.

In her book *Without Child,* Laurie Lisle noted that "liberal or idealistic men who believe in gender equality or co-parenting are sometimes more reluctant to undertake fatherhood than traditional males who feel no obligation to share child care.

Opting for childlessness often seems more honorable to many of them than taking on a half-hearted or irresponsible fatherhood."[5] Indeed, in my own interviews with couples, I saw evidence of this way of thinking: The men seemed to consider their perceived lack of paternal instinct or desire in the context of its impact on a future child. Women did, too, but they also saw that lack as problematic because they considered instinct and desire to be critical assets in child rearing.

MOTIVE STATEMENT 5:
I WANT TO ACCOMPLISH/EXPERIENCE THINGS IN LIFE THAT WOULD BE DIFFICULT TO DO IF I WAS A PARENT.

Initially, I assumed that more women than men would identify strongly with this statement. However, the opposite proved true: 68 percent of the men rated this statement a 4 or 5, compared with 62 percent of the women.

Jodi, who had helped raise her younger sibling, valued her newfound freedom. "Basically, it comes down to being able to do just about anything we want without having to consider the needs of anyone else. As care providers when we were younger, neither my husband nor I got to experience this until recently."

Many couples had some basis for comparison between times when they were free to take advantage of opportunities and times when they were tied down by obligations. Among the survey respondents, 64 percent felt compelled to remain childless partly because some of their dreams and goals would be difficult, if not impossible, to accomplish if they took on the responsibilities of parenthood.

"I worked full-time, and I would have felt too guilty to put my kids in daycare," said Sue, knowing that she would have prioritized childcare responsibilities over her career and educational goals. "If I'd had a child in my early twenties, it would have been difficult, because of time and money, to attend graduate school or to pursue any kind of continuing education later in life."

Lou, a retired military man, treasured his memories of trips he and his wife had taken when they lived overseas. "We have traveled the world and have seen things that most people with children can't afford to do until they retire," Lou wrote in his questionnaire. His wife, Jessica, became disabled by chronic pain in her forties and had very limited mobility when I interviewed them. "It was the best thing we ever did with our life—to travel when we were young and healthy. We were freer then—emotionally, psychologically, and financially," Lou told me.

MOTIVE STATEMENT 6:
I WANT TO FOCUS MY TIME AND ENERGY ON MY OWN INTERESTS, NEEDS, OR GOALS.

Behind this motive statement is the assumption that specific personal needs and goals cannot be met or achieved when a person makes the huge time commitment required to raise children. It is, in a sense, a rejection of the idea that you can do it all—at least successfully.

Claudia saw the tradeoffs and credited her successful career to "being able to really focus on work, going up the corporate ladder, and being very flexible." She felt it was necessary to "put in the extra hours to make those kinds of things happen. Those things wouldn't have happened if we had a family."

Gina wanted to start her own business. Her father was an entrepreneur and she knew firsthand the time and dedication running a business required. "If you're going to have a successful business you have to pour yourself into it. If I could have one criticism of him as a father, that would be it, that he really did have so much going on that we missed out on having him as a father."

Sara recognized that remaining childless "gives us a little more freedom to work toward our goals. We can concentrate our time and energy not only on making our marriage better, but on growing and learning as individuals and becoming better people."

Gina and Sara were under the age of thirty-five at the time of our interview. Respondents aged twenty to twenty-nine strongly identified with this motive statement: 71 percent rated it a 4 or 5, compared with only 42 percent of the fifty-and-older group. As a whole, 60 percent of the survey respondents strongly identified with this statement, showing a strong predisposition to allocate some energy for personal needs and goals.

Can we do it all? Or are resources, like time and energy, finite to the extent that we must prioritize those things that we feel are important to us? At least for those who strongly identified with this motive statement, goals, interests, and needs did not include parenthood at this point in their lives.

MOTIVE STATEMENT 7:
THE COSTS OUTWEIGH THE BENEFITS, FINANCIALLY AND OTHERWISE.

In her study entitled "Choosing Childlessness: Weber's Typology of Action and Motives of the Voluntarily Childless," Dr. Kristin Park observed that "men more than women framed their childless decision in terms of explicit cost-benefit analyses in which the benefits of parenting were overridden by its direct and opportunity costs, including financial expense."[6]

In my survey, however, 58 percent of the women strongly identified with this statement, compared with 48 percent of the men.

Jacqui, along with her fiancé, had weighed the benefits and costs with the awareness that "kids cost an enormous amount of money." She recalled her mother's experience in a "horrible" marriage precipitated by an out-of-wedlock birth. She imagined that the costs of being a parent would be equally miserable, punctuated by chronic sleep deprivation and stress. She wanted the benefit and "the freedom to be able to work a sixty-hour-per-week job that involves monthly travel, and not worry about someone being dependent on me."

On one level, Donna's choice to remain childless was purely pragmatic. "When Ed and I were first married, we simply didn't have enough money to raise a child responsibly," wrote Donna. Then, after many years in a childfree marriage, Donna acknowledged another level of intention and motives: "I'm so grateful for all that we have, and I simply don't want to change our lifestyle."

Ditto for Mark and his wife, Debb: "When we were in our twenties and thirties, there were real financial issues. I realize that many people with little income do indeed have children, but it seemed for me that bringing a child into that situation would have made life very difficult for all involved. At this time, financially, I could consider being a parent, but it is not something that I feel I must have to make my life complete."

Some of the couples who identified with this statement postponed children because they couldn't afford them, and then decided to remain childfree. Others had weighed the risks, or costs, of parenthood and found them unacceptable, given what the couple currently enjoyed and valued about their life.

MOTIVE STATEMENT 8:
I CAN SERVE MYSELF BETTER BY
NOT HAVING CHILDREN.

This motive actually tied with motive statement 7 as the seventh-most-compelling motive for the group. Women, more than men, strongly identified with this statement: 58 percent of the women and 48 percent of the men I surveyed rated this statement a 4 or 5.

Tamara saw a new generation of mothers who "have an intensity about raising their children that really pushes them back into roles where they have absolutely no power. There are women who are like, *I am going to be empowered—I'm going to have a career; I'm going to be empowered—I choose to have a child; I'm going to be empowered—I choose to stay home.* But then it's *Oh, wait a minute, my husband just left me and now I have no power, no money, my kid is being torn apart, I'm working all the time, and I am in abject poverty.*"

Some of the people I encountered spoke of a need for self-healing or self-parenting work before they even thought about having a child of their own. They believed that their health and well-being were works in progress, or fragile, and that the introduction of a dependent child into their life might risk undoing some of that work or leave little time or resources to continue those efforts.

Grace wrote, "I've been able to spend most of my life on personal and spiritual development, and this is what I provide to others now. I work as a mediator and a certified mentor. I volunteer as a legal advocate for people seeking restraining orders, and I teach workshops in personal and spiritual development. My upbringing and marriage left a lot to be desired, and I've had to spend a lot of my life 'fixing' myself after these long-term disasters. I barely found myself as it was, and with kids, I probably never would have."

Most of us are influenced by the experiences of friends and family members, whether we like it or not. In our attempts to empathize with parents, we sometimes project our own reactions onto their experiences. My respondents who were aware of having done this often found that it helped them come to the conclusion that they would not enjoy being a parent. Choosing to remain childless was a way to protect themselves from what they imagined to be a future of stress, anguish, or powerlessness.

MOTIVE STATEMENT 9:
I AM CONCERNED ABOUT THE STATE OF OUR WORLD, AND I DO NOT THINK IT WOULD BE WISE TO BRING A CHILD INTO IT.

Although this was not one of the most compelling motives for the majority of those surveyed, 49 percent of the group strongly identified with this statement. In my conversations with childless by choice couples, many of them expressed how difficult they felt it would be to raise a child in today's society.

"I don't see any truly safe place for children," said Damian. "I would be scared to death to let them go to school, and you can't turn on the TV without seeing sex, drugs, and violence. Some of the things that were in place to keep children safe are gone." What he saw instead was more crime and fear.

Jacqui wrote, "It is difficult to raise children well in this materialistic and instant-gratification society." Her fiancé, Louis, concurred: "This is not the same place I grew up in, and I don't believe I would be comfortable bringing a child into it."

Many parents living in the United States agree with these statements and share those fears. In a Public Agenda report titled "A Lot Easier Said Than Done," a majority of parents felt, as paraphrased by researchers, that "American society is an inhospitable climate for raising children, where parents can never let down their guard in the face of popular culture, drugs and crime. In fact, nearly half the parents we surveyed said they worry more about protecting their child from negative social influences than about paying the bills or having enough family time together. Six in ten rate their generation 'fair' or 'poor' in raising children."[7]

Theresa's identification with this motive statement had to do with the environment: "I would feel guilty bringing another person into this world knowing they would have to clean up what the rest of us have left behind."

It's disheartening to note that both parents and nonparents agree that our current environment is inhospitable to children. Fear is the common emotion here; parents are acknowledging that they live with it, and nonparents are saying they would rather not have to.

MOTIVE STATEMENT 10:
I CAN BETTER SERVE THE WORLD BY
NOT HAVING CHILDREN.

Altruistic motives for childlessness ranged from being able to pursue careers that would be of service to others to making a commitment to the environment or to helping children. Quite a few of the childfree people I spoke with had taught or mentored youth or worked with charities that served underprivileged families and children. Many of them felt that they could do more as nonparents to help improve the lives of others.

Manmeet was a community activist and was one of the undecided respondents: "Actually," he told me during our interview, "in the first year or two of our marriage, we did talk about having children, but as we got focused on ourselves and the bigger picture, we thought our contribution would be to leave nothing behind and yet do our best to make the world a better place." Although he had not ruled out having children at some point, he said, "We remain childless so we can work on projects that will help children and communities."

According to Anthony, an active-duty army officer, "I am of greater benefit to society and my country by remaining childfree and concentrating my efforts on service, and duty to my country."

Other participants were not convinced the world is in desperate need of another person carrying their DNA. "I can do more for society and the planet by not making copies of myself," said Jerry, who believed his work teaching English to immigrants was more important than contributing one more native-born person to Canada.

Trond likes kids and was working at a daycare center when I interviewed him. "As a hardcore environmentalist in my late twenties," he told me, "I couldn't see myself adding to the pressures on the planet with a clear conscience." His wife, Roz, was similarly motivated: "Originally it was a very political choice, since I felt the earth had way too many human beings, so why bring in more garbage-producing consumers? As much as I love the potentiality of a newborn, I have to say that I still feel pretty much the same way as I did ten years ago."

Rachel believed that "remaining childfree is the single largest environmental contribution anyone can make." Elaine agreed: "Many of the problems that we have now can be traced to overpopulation, on both a domestic and a global scale. Reproducing would be just plain ego masturbation, given the current population circumstances."

Less than half of my respondents rated the statement "I can better serve the world by not having children" a 4 or 5, but those who did expressed strong views. Initially, I suspected that those who were motivated to remain childfree by environmental concerns might have been raised during the '60s and '70s, but this turned out not to be the case. Though age groups who identified with this statement were comparable, the twenty-to-twenty-nine age group was more inclined to identify with this motive statement than the forty-to-forty-nine age group was.

MOTIVE STATEMENT 11:
MY LIFESTYLE/CAREER IS INCOMPATIBLE WITH
RAISING CHILDREN.

Scratch the surface of the primary motives, and you'll often find childfree men and women engaged in demanding or creative work that requires more than a nine-to-five commitment, or in jobs that require traveling away from home. What comes first—the incompatible lifestyle or the decision not to have kids? Is it the job or the lifestyle that prompts someone to remain childless, or does the choice to remain childless free a person to engage in work or activities that demand this kind of time and energy? I'm not sure.

Harpreet was focusing her energies on a career in filmmaking, using her talents to expose genocide and human-rights abuses. "I want to do something meaningful in my life. I'm twenty-eight, and I don't think I've done anything at the level where I'm satisfied. The career I'm in requires a lot of time and travel. If I decide to be a mother, I want to be able to be there for my child. I can't give my career a halfhearted effort and commitment, and I can't do that to my child, either."

Quite a few of the people Dr. Kristin Park surveyed for her research on the motives of the voluntarily childless were in the academic community. She noted, "It is very difficult for mothers in academia, because the child-bearing years coincide, oftentimes, with years where you are expected to be working sixty hour weeks towards tenure."[8]

Laurie Lisle, author of *Without Child,* noted that people engaged in creative endeavors perceived they could not do what they did and parent effectively at the same time. "Men and women without children also tell interviewers about their passionate involvement in original work that demands inspiration and inventiveness, as well as many hours alone. Such absorption is antithetical to the activities involved in taking care of a family. In fact, the creative process often needs to be protected and nurtured much the way a child does."[9]

Although the majority of my survey respondents (including me) did not feel this statement was the most compelling motive for them, I could identify with it because I had chosen to marry a career-driven man. My husband was among the 45 percent who strongly identified with this statement, and wrote (in the questionnaire I made him fill out), "Having children would have adversely affected my career growth possibilities, and would not have allowed me to be as independent as I have been, or allowed me to take the risks in life that I have taken."

I am attracted to my husband, Robert, because he is a hard-working entrepreneur and a risk taker who enjoys traveling the world. Early in our marriage, he was working in international sales and traveling overseas as many as six months of the year. Had we had a child, his absence would have made me a de facto single mom in the days before Skype, cell phones, and email. Thankfully, neither of us wanted to start a family, which enabled us to pursue the careers we wanted.

MOTIVE STATEMENT 12:
I HAVE SEEN OR EXPERIENCED FIRSTHAND THE EFFECTS OF BAD OR UNINTENTIONAL PARENTING, AND I DON'T WANT TO RISK THE CHANCE THAT I MIGHT PERPETUATE THAT SITUATION.

I have often been asked if this statement was the primary reason why people choose not to have kids. And I have to tell them no. Of the people I surveyed, less than 42 percent were strongly compelled to remain childless for this reason.

Although the response to this statement wasn't over-whelming, quite a few of the people I interviewed spoke, on and off the record, about having had a difficult or neglected childhood. Many of them felt that their parents were emotion-ally or temperamentally ill equipped to raise children. Some spoke about peers or relatives they described as "bad" parents and expressed fear that they might not do any better. Almost all of the childless by choice people I spoke with believed that certain people should not be encouraged to parent—for the sake of the children.

"I came from a tense and intense family that seemed de-void of joy," acknowledged Grace. "Childhood was not a fun, expressive experience for me, and I never felt my parents en-joyed raising us very much, either. I found out later that my mother had not especially wanted children, nor had her moth-er before her."

Jessica's heart told her something was seriously wrong with her family, but she didn't have the words to express what it was until she went to college. "I experienced bad parenting with my father's verbal belittling, and my mother not protect-ing me from my father's verbal onslaughts. My father told me, on my twenty-fifth birthday, 'You can die, for all I care—you're not worth the air I breathe.' And my mother didn't do anything to stop or correct him. In 1979, when I started my master's de-gree in counseling and human development, the term 'dysfunc-tional family' was unknown to me. As I started into the course program, I discovered that, lo and behold, I was from one of the most dysfunctional families on Earth. I was horrified. I ac-tually became afraid that if I were to have children, I would continue the cycle of emotional and verbal abuse."

Like Jessica, some people see how unhappy parents can raise unhappy children. If they believe that good parenting springs from a combination of desire, skill, and good role models, and if they determine they have none of the above in sufficient quantities, they may feel impelled to opt out of parenthood.

MOTIVE STATEMENT 13:
I DON'T ENJOY BEING AROUND CHILDREN.

Again, contrary to my assumptions going into this project, I found more women than men who were willing to admit they don't enjoy prolonged exposure to children. Of the women I surveyed, 46 percent strongly identified with this statement, compared with 32 percent of the men. Early articulators of both genders are also more likely to acknowledge that children, particularly dependent infants, do not appeal to them. Many early-articulating women also recalled a "dislike" of dolls and of playing house.

Kevin was "never really fond of children." He noted that exposure to children usually left him feeling "annoyed," and he came to believe that "not everyone is suited to have children, and I am not, in so many ways."

Kevin's partner, Misty, had chosen not to have kids mainly because "I don't enjoy being around children. Why would someone do something they hated? Or, even worse, subject an innocent human life to a parent who resented them and didn't like them? That would be cruel!"

"I never enjoyed kids, even when I was a kid," said Elaine. "My mom always told me that although she liked being a parent, it wasn't for everyone, and with the advent of birth control, there was no excuse for accidental pregnancies. She worked in a hospital for a while, and she would tell of abused children who would come through the emergency room having 'fallen off their bike.' Her message was 'When in doubt, don't have kids.'"

In his survey of the childfree, Vincent Ciaccio found that the majority of the women preferred to be around older children or teenagers rather than toddlers and infants, a finding that prompted him to remark, "The belief that all women are automatically enamored with babies is unsubstantiated."[10] In our profamily culture, it takes a certain amount of candor to admit that you don't enjoy being around children. I believe that because my respondents knew I, too, was childless by choice, they felt safe telling me this. It is also easier to be honest if your partner knows how you feel and is okay with it.

MOTIVE STATEMENT 14:
MY PARTNER DOESN'T WANT KIDS.

It's important to note that the vast majority of the 41 percent of people who cite this as a compelling motive acknowledge that they, too, are ambivalent about having children. Although they explain that their choice to remain childless was influenced by their partner's choice, they say that if they'd really felt a strong urge to have kids, they wouldn't have chosen to stay in the relationship. Madelyn Cain called these folks Childless by Marriage and, in her book *The Childless Revolution,* noted a tinge of regret from a woman who had acquiesced to a life without kids.[11] Because most of the acquiescers I interviewed were male, I didn't have a big enough sample of female acquiescers to draw any conclusions; however, I did not see any evidence of regret in either gender.

Kathryn told Mike on their first date that she didn't want to have kids, in the spirit of full disclosure. This forced him to explore his own feelings about parenthood. "I had never really thought of it that much until I met Kathryn. It wasn't until then I realized what an important decision it was to make and, once I put serious thought into it, I realized 110 percent that I did not want to have a child."

"Before age twenty-seven, I assumed I would become a parent," wrote Lou. "Then, during Army service in 1982, I met

Jessica and she told me that she was not at all interested in having children. Before I committed to Jessica, I spent a few months researching parenthood through the eyes of other soldiers in my unit. Although most of the soldiers admitted they loved their children, they also spoke of constant financial and emotional conflicts, as well as being physically drained from the constant needs of their children. That's when I decided that not having children might be a good thing."

I was struck by all the men who admitted they had never considered the possibility of a life without children until their girlfriends announced their desire to remain childless. However, once they entertained the idea, they realized how completely onboard they were. Lou confirmed that when I asked: "Yes," he said, "Jessica influenced me to consider remaining childless, and then I discovered it was my own preference."

Mitch came to appreciate the benefits of a childfree marriage the longer he went without having children: "I chose to remain childfree initially because my wife did not want children. After being married a few years, I was not willing to give up the freedom of being childfree."

Sean's wife, Nancy, challenged him to question his motives for parenthood. "Nancy always stated that she did not want children, and did question my reasoning for having kids, which made me question myself about it. My reasons to have children were to carry on the family name, and because I thought that I would need someone to take care of me during my senior years."

In the questionnaire, Nancy recalled her own feelings at that time: "When Sean and I were dating, he used to hear me say that I did not want children, but he thought that my beliefs were a passing phase. After a year into our marriage, Sean and I realized that we had differing views about children. I was prepared, due to my love for him, to consider having one child for Sean's sake. Thankfully, Sean came to his own realization about children, and we never had to compromise our relationship in such a drastic manner."

Nancy and Sean were fortunate to eventually arrive at a meeting of the minds about children. Even before I began my research, I had heard about couples who'd broken up because one partner wanted kids and the other didn't, so initially I feared for the acquiescers—would they continue to feel content with their decision? Later, I would begin to understand that most of those who identified as acquiescers did not feel they were in any way coerced into a childfree marriage; most of them said only that their partner's desires prompted a personal process of discernment, a process that might not have occurred otherwise.

MOTIVE STATEMENT 15:
I DON'T THINK I WOULD MAKE A GOOD PARENT.

Only 26 percent of the men and 30 percent of the women I surveyed were strongly compelled to remain childfree because of a perceived lack of parenting skills or aptitude. This issue seems to be a very nuanced one, as the bulk of my interview subjects discussed this motive within the context of choice, which may be the ideal, but not always the reality, for the childless by choice. For instance, though many couples visibly shuddered when I asked them to imagine themselves parenting a child, they also said they would of course try to be the best parents they could be if they were to get pregnant accidentally. Yet those who cited this as a compelling motive truly doubted their ability to succeed as a parent, even with good intentions. As Lou said in my interview with him, "I'd really have to force it to be a good dad."

Elaine wrote, "I took a hard look at my temperament, personality, goals, and desires and realized a child probably wouldn't be too happy being raised by someone like me."

"I've got an incredibly short temper. My father did as well," said Damian. "I can't imagine being that enraged around a child. It's scary." His wife, Kathleen, agreed, and had this to say about herself: "I'm very obsessive and compulsive; I'm the triple-checker. I see myself being the parent that's just over-bearing and awake all night worrying."

For Jodi, "I don't think I would make a good parent" seemed like a gross understatement. "Oh, I would be a terrible parent," she confessed. "If the rating of five is indicative of being the antichrist of parents, that would be me. I'd be an angry, remote, and resentful mother."

It's hard to admit that you think you wouldn't make a good parent, and I had to admire the honesty of these men and women. They had obviously thought a great deal about their ability to parent, and had declared themselves unfit. I couldn't help but think, *Wouldn't it be a revolutionary thing if we all did this?*

MOTIVE STATEMENT 16:
PEOPLE I KNOW HAVE NOT REALIZED THE REWARDS THEY EXPECTED AS A PARENT.

Is parenthood a rewarding experience? If you believe you will go through the experience of raising children and look back and say, "In the end, it was worth all of the grief and head-aches," then it definitely is. But what if the joys of parenthood are not readily apparent to you?

Only 30 percent of the men and 25 percent of the women I surveyed strongly identified with this statement—perhaps because so many of us know people who appear to be happy and fulfilled as parents. We hear things like "Raising kids is hell sometimes, but in the end it's so worth it." Still, some of us don't believe we would feel this way. Others, like Patrick, suspected that parents put on a happy face just to fool them: "We're suffering—you suffer too." Misery loves company.

Are parents engaging in what Susan Jeffers called a "conspiracy of silence"?

Some are, some are not. We hear parents touting the blessings of parenthood, and then we read that back in 1975, when advice columnist Ann Landers asked parents if they would choose to have kids again, given what they know now, 70 percent of her respondents said no. Not that we really need Ann Landers to tell us that some parents are regretful—if you're a child of a regretful parent, you just know, even when the parent doesn't verbalize it. If you disclose the fact that you are childless by choice in a room full of parents, you're likely to hear some variation on the message "You're smart—if I could return my kids to the store, I would." Sometimes it's said in jest and sometimes it's not. However, the message is the same: Parenthood is not always as advertised, so buyers beware.

Jeff had "personally known several couples who never truly realized the rewards they expected as a parent. This was mostly due to the fact that they had a child with a serious disability, like cerebral palsy and spina bifida. These couples had the normal expectations during their pregnancy but were utterly devastated shortly after their children were born with these crippling conditions. They have privately confided to me that although they love their children, they are sometimes sorry they went down the road to parenthood in the first place."

Jeff, who postponed parenthood prior to embracing his childfree life, was also influenced by the many still-dependent adults he saw around him. "My brother-in-law has gone his whole life with undiagnosed ADD, and I see the problems it has created for him. My wife and I realize his disability and help him out regularly, financially and otherwise, but he will need some form of assistance for the rest of his life."

Jeff is someone who's witnessed how others have dealt with some pretty tough realities, and has decided for himself that it's not worth the risk.

Other people I spoke with suspected the regret and disappointment some parents express had less to do with their children and more to do with their high expectations going into parenthood. When expectations are high, parenthood can seem like a bait-and-switch scheme. The gap between what people imagine or anticipate and the reality they experience can be huge, leaving some parents to wonder—sometimes out loud—how they were duped.

MOTIVE STATEMENT 17:
I DELAYED HAVING CHILDREN AND EVENTUALLY DECIDED I WANTED TO REMAIN CHILDLESS.

Only 21 percent of women and 22 percent of men gave this statement a rating of 4 or 5. This was not surprising, as only 21 percent of the survey respondents described themselves as postponers. The rest of the survey respondents had decided early in adulthood to remain childless, had acquiesced to a partner's wish to remain childfree, or were undecided.

The majority of the postponers I spoke with went into their relationships thinking that they would have children, but then chose to delay parenthood. They wanted time as a couple, time to establish themselves in a career, or time to feel more emotionally ready or more financially secure. Some had agreed upon a deadline, or had simply continued to delay having kids until they'd reached a point at which they'd decided they really didn't want or need children of their own.

Early in her marriage, Kathy entertained the idea of having children, even though she expressed that she didn't think she would be happy as a mother. She thought these feelings would change with time. "I always thought I would eventually want them, but the desire never surfaced."

Mark and Debb assumed they would have children, but early in their marriage, kids weren't an option for them financially. They debated the pros and cons of parenthood for years, until they decided they would remain childfree, and ultimately Mark's vasectomy marked the end point of an intense process of discernment.

MOTIVE STATEMENT 18:
I AM CONCERNED ABOUT THE PHYSICAL RISKS OF CHILDBIRTH AND RECOVERY.

Predictably, more women than men were motivated by the physical risks of childbirth. Many of the women who did identify with this statement expressed fear of the risks of childbirth due to preexisting health conditions that might complicate their pregnancy or jeopardize their health. A few cited a low tolerance for pain or a family history of postpartum depression as the main reason for their fear. Both men and women worried about the risk of complications during delivery, or possible long-term health effects.

Even so, only 24 percent of the women and 12 percent of the men rated this statement a 4 or a 5, forcing it to the bottom of the list of the most compelling motives and effectively dispelling the notion that childfree women make this choice because they are worried about their waistline. However, it is interesting that 12 percent of the men surveyed rated this statement a 4 or a 5, indicating that a small but significant number of childfree men are concerned about the risks of childbirth and recovery, too.

THE CHILDFREE FOR NOW

You may be thinking, *Gosh, I'm nothing like these people. These motives have never even crossed my mind. Yet I've remained childless, so what's that all about?* Or maybe you are looking at these motives and thinking, *Yes, I really do share a lot of these motives, but I still want to have a child.*

You are not alone.

Let's use the example of Patrick and Tara, the undecided couple from Chapter 3 who allowed me to document their decision-making process. Tara felt awkward around kids. She didn't feel maternal and didn't believe in maternal instinct. Period. Patrick valued his freedom and knew that if he had a child, "everything would change." He loved his life the way it was, and was "not that excited to change it."

Yet despite identifying with most of the top motives to remain childfree, they still ultimately chose to have a child together. I spoke with them as I was writing this chapter, a few months after their son's first birthday. They'd had a couple of rough months after his birth but had settled into a routine in which they were both working out of their home, sharing child-rearing responsibilities, and making time for some outside interests, and they were clearly happy with their choice.

So if it is possible to live happily childfree and happily with children, then how do you know what is the right choice for you? Richard didn't think it was wise, or necessary, to attach relative values to parenthood or nonparenthood. "I don't think it's a comparative state of better or worse; I just think it's a decision we made."

That's true—there is no "right" choice. However, if you are on the fence, it may help you to look to those who have made the choice to remain childless, as a way to gauge your own feelings and intuition. I asked my participants to offer suggestions or questions that might help others in their decision-making process.

THE "KIDS OR NO KIDS?" TEST

Are you childfree by choice, or just postponing parenthood?

A year or so ago, I was in a noisy bar with a former co-worker of my husband's who was in her late thirties and had previously tried to conceive without success. Her husband was ambivalent about children but was willing to be a dad if it happened. They were considering fertility treatments, and she wondered if it was going to be worth all the stress and expense, or if she could be happy without kids. She clearly wanted my opinion.

I told her about the undecided couples I had interviewed, asked a few indirect questions, and then sat back and listened, trying to determine how she might have responded to these more direct questions:

- Do I really want to be a parent?
- Do I enjoy children?
- Will I likely regret it if I don't have kids?

After listening to her responses, I said, "Yes, I think you should try to have a kid." I recently found out that she and her husband were expecting a child, thanks to in vitro fertilization.

Participants in the Childless by Choice Project had asked themselves these types of questions in the course of their decision making, and I invited them to share their questions with others who were wondering if they were ready and willing to be a parent.

Rachael suggested asking yourself this question: Do I have close friends who are pregnant or who have small children? If so, am I envious of their lifestyle or apprehensive about how I would handle it?

Jennifer asked: "Are you having kids because you think that is 'the next step' in life, or are you making the choice to have kids because you truly want to share your life with a new generation?"

Anthony, who was trained by the U.S. Army to think in terms of resources and skill sets, suggested, "Take a personal inventory of your level of responsibility, discipline, and well-being. Have a solid financial base and belief structure, then decide whether or not to have children."

Sue, who holds a master's in counseling psychology, suggested putting it to paper. "List the pros and cons of having children—what are the advantages, disadvantages? What skills do you have to raise a healthy, well-adjusted child to adulthood? How would the way you and your partner were raised by your own parents affect your parenting style?"

Jerry suggested a drill to test your willingness to make the changes necessary to parent: "At least twenty times a day for the next week or month, ask yourself the following question: How would having children change what I am doing now? Ask it when you wake up, when you eat your meals, when you watch TV, when you read the newspaper, when you walk the dog, when you make love, when you go to sleep. If you consider most of your answers to be positive, then you might enjoy having children. If most of your answers are negative, then you might be happier without children of your own."

Ed suggested the puppy test: "Get a puppy first. If you can train it well and give it the time it deserves (not kennel it every other weekend), and it becomes a loving, happy dog, you're likely ready to have kids, and if you still want to have kids after having the puppy, then by all means, have them."

"This isn't a snap decision; it should take a lot of soul searching," Vincent said, and suggested that the soul searching include the question "Am I prepared to have a child that isn't 'perfect'? This includes the possibilities of mental and physical disabilities."

Often the "perfect" child is imagined as a cute little potato-head doll with Daddy's eyes and Mommy's nose. John and Kathy wondered why people are so hung up on having a biological child—do they really want the experience of raising a child, or do they want a "mini-me"? They suggested you ask yourself whether, if you and your partner were unable to have a child of your own, you would adopt.

Laura and Dan felt that to be true to themselves, to be authentic, they had to listen to their gut and remain childfree.

So how do you know what your gut wants? Easy: Spend a couple of quiet moments alone, imagining yourself as a parent. What does that feel like? Is it an excited, warm-and-fuzzy feeling, or does it feel wrong, uncomfortable, or even impossible? Some fear is natural when you imagine what will probably be one of the toughest responsibilities you ever take on. However, if imagining yourself in a mom or dad role feels really foreign or unnatural or totally uncharacteristic for you, you might want to take the time to reread this book and think hard about what you really want and what you really feel.

UNDERSTANDING THE NUMBERS

As is the case with any survey, individual respondents' ratings are pooled to determine values and frequencies for the group as a whole. So even though my respondents rated the potential physical risks of childbirth and recovery as the least compelling reason cumulatively, you as an individual may have given this a 5 rating, and that's perfectly valid, too. The truth is that all of these statements ranked highest for some of the participants. And all of the motive statements are equally legitimate in the sense that each one has influenced the decision-making process of the childfree by choice.

The decision to remain childless is made by one person or one couple at a time. The millions of people who make this choice do so for many reasons, with influences and ideals too diverse and complex to cram into a list. All of the respondents in the Childless by Choice Project survey strongly identified with at least three of the eighteen motives listed above. Some decided in their teens to remain childfree, while others did so in their thirties, after years of assuming they would be parents one day.

In my survey sample of 171 self-selected respondents, 66 percent were early articulators. I doubt that percentage would apply to the entire voluntarily childless population in North America. At first, I didn't think much about the fact that so many of my participants described themselves as early articulators. In fact, given the way I went about getting my respondents, I had expected this to be the case. Those who identify as intentionally childless from an early point in their lives are more likely to have done the work of assimilating this aspect of themselves into their identity, and are therefore more likely to sign up to participate in a project like mine. However, when I went to do the statistical analysis, I worried that the ratings from this large percentage of early articulators would skew the results for the other groups. What I found instead was that most of the top six motives for this group also showed up in the list of the top six motives for each of the other decision-making categories.

Another reason why I might have had so many early articulators as respondents is that I purposely did not stipulate an age by which they would have had to decide to remain childfree for them to qualify as early articulators. This was intentional because I wanted to explore the decision to remain childless as both a choice and a process; I knew that some people who would self-identify as early articulators—based on the fact that early in their lives, they expressed a desire to remain childless—would also acknowledge having undergone a decision-making process that occupied as many as ten years.

Some studies have defined early articulators—or, even more broadly, the intentionally childless—as those who decide or publicly articulate by age eighteen, twenty, or twenty-five that they will remain childless. Based on my research and reading, I did not think this criterion was wise, given that many young people do not feel empowered, in a culture that assumes parenthood for all, to speak out about or act on their desire to remain childless.

MOTIVES BY GENDER

Before I analyzed the data, I assumed the women's top motives would be very different from the men's. Wrong again. When Dr. Houston and I analyzed the motive statements by gender, we found that the top five most compelling motives were shared by over 60 percent of the whole group, regardless of their gender.

Women were more likely than men to give a high rating to the statement "I have no desire to have a child, no maternal/ paternal instinct"; 75 percent of women rated it a 4 or 5, compared with 64 percent of men.

Though men were more likely than women to strongly identify with the statements "I love our life, our relationship, as it is, and having a child won't enhance it" (78 percent of men and 68 percent of women) and "I don't want to take on the responsibility of raising a child" (82 percent of men and 70 percent of women), I was surprised by the extent to which the men and women agreed on what the five most compelling motives to remain childfree were.

MOTIVES BY AGE

Where motives differed significantly was in the age groups I surveyed. Those aged 20–29 were much more likely than the 50-and-older group to strongly identify with "I value freedom and independence": A full 100 percent of the 20–29 group rated this statement a 4 or 5, compared with only 61 percent of the 50-and-older group. Another big gap showed up in the age analysis of "I want to focus my time and energy on my own interests, needs, or goals": 71 percent of the 20–29 age group strongly identified with this statement, while only 42 percent of the 50-and-older group did.

The 40–49 age group was much more likely to be motivated by the statement "I am concerned about the state of our world, and I do not think it would be wise to bring a child into it" than the 20–29 age group was: 58 percent of the former group rated this statement a 4 or 5, compared with 29 percent of the latter group. The 40–49 group was also significantly more likely to be motivated by the statement "The costs outweigh the benefits, financially and otherwise" than was the 50-and-older group: 63 percent of the former group strongly identified with this statement, compared with 39 percent of the latter group.

Why these disparities by age? I suspect that the twenty- to twenty-nine-year-olds who identified with the statement "I want to focus my time and energy on my own interests, needs, or goals" were in the midst of sequencing their priorities and parenthood was, at that moment, low on their list. I don't think I am being judgmental when I say that twenty-year-olds, whether they have children or not, tend to be more self-focused than fifty-year-olds; I think most people would agree with this assessment.

MOTIVES BY DECISION-MAKING CATEGORY

Much like the analysis we did on the top motives by gender, the analysis of motives by decision-making category revealed that early articulators, postponers, and acquiescers strongly identified with at least four of the top six motives for the whole group. The only exception to this broad agreement among the decision-making groups were the acquiescers, those people who were influenced by their partner to remain childless; only 47 percent gave a 4 or 5 rating to "I have no desire to have a child, no maternal/paternal instinct," while 79 percent of the early articulators and 65 percent of the postponers did.

However, 100 percent of the acquiescers who were in a committed partnership gave a 4 or 5 rating to the statement "I love our life, our relationship as it is, and having a child won't enhance it." This finding was important because it showed that even those who'd anticipated children for themselves, or may have felt an affinity for children, could transition to a childfree life successfully and happily.

WHAT THE NUMBERS TELL US

Some of my data analysis challenged my assumptions, particularly about gender. I found that more women than I would have predicted were motivated by a lack of desire for children and a perceived lack of maternal instinct. I saw men and women in agreement on the high value they placed on their freedom and independence, and on their childfree life and relationships.

I noted that some of the reasons that society assumes the childless by choice have for their intentional childlessness—like an aversion to children, a bad childhood, or concerns about childbirth and recovery—did not make the list of the top six most compelling motives among my respondents.

I also saw similarities between my survey and surveys of the childfree that had come before mine, which suggested that the top motives people cited in the '70s and '80s—such as marital satisfaction and the freedom to pursue opportunities, which respondents felt were important for their happiness and sense of fulfillment—are as compelling today as they were thirty years ago.

I was also surprised and delighted to see that my personal motives for remaining childless were represented in the top six most compelling motives, erasing any doubt I might have harbored about their validity and the degree to which others share them.

CHAPTER 5

On the Same Page:
Soul Mates, Partners, and Best Friends

When I first began pitching this book to agents and publishers, I was gripped by the irrational fear that my husband would suddenly admit to me that he actually did want kids after all. I imagined being on a radio show, promoting the book, and taking a call from a woman claiming to be the mother of his love child, sentencing me to a lifetime of guilt for ignoring his needs and exposing our happily childfree marriage as a lie.

But on the nights when we sit on our deck, watching the sun go down, and he expresses how much he enjoys these quiet, peaceful moments and the benefits of a childfree life, all such fears vanish; I know that we are on the same page and that the decision we made was right for both of us.

During the months when I traveled around North America, interviewing childless by choice couples, I began to wonder if they were reading from a common script. A suspiciously high number independently expressed relief that they were "on the same page." As I heard these exact words repeated time after time, I overcame my skepticism and embraced the fact that those of us who enter into a partnership with someone who shares our goals and values do, in fact, feel an overwhelming sense of gratitude. On this one gargantuan issue—parenthood—my partner and I had agreed. How tragic would it have been had we not?

For me, it would have meant risking losing my best friend, my other half. As my intentionally childless marriage implies, I value a strong and enduring relationship with a life partner more than I do the prospect of parenthood, but I can certainly empathize with those who desire a child above all else, because I can't imagine how Robert and I would manage if one of us were to change our mind. Failure to agree on the issue of kids can be a deal breaker for couples; at best, it presents a life-altering challenge that likely requires negotiation, compromise, and more than a few sessions of couples' therapy to address the real possibility of regret or resentment. For me, a workable compromise on something as huge as parenthood seemed impossible.

So how do couples come to this agreement—on the first date, or after five years together? Both, as it turns out. And what happens after that? They agree to a life without children. What does that look like? What are the benefits and the downsides? What happens when you get old?

I wanted answers to these and other questions, and to find them I needed to go beyond the questionnaires and interview childless by choice couples in committed partnerships to better understand how these relationships had been forged, and how they functioned and endured. To prepare for these interviews, I worked from a menu of standard questions designed to explore how the couples had begun to consider a childfree life: their first "kid conversation"; their motivations; their decision-making process; how their families had responded; how they managed the pressure, stigmas, and assumptions; and how they perceived their relationship.

I wanted to know what these couples had experienced as the pros and cons of a life without biological children, and what they wanted me, and the readers of this book, to know about their decision and their lives.

Below are seven couples' stories, chosen for their diversity of experience. All these couples were in their thirties and early forties when I interviewed them. I was interested in this specific age range because it's a time when couples still experience pressure to have kids, and when the details and the perceived and actual consequences of their decision making are still fresh in their minds.

MICHELLE AND NAJI

Michelle and her husband, Naji, are both early articulators who had built a life together on a foundation of friendship. When I interviewed them, they were thirty-seven and forty-three, respectively, and had been married for fifteen years.

They first met when Naji hired Michelle to work in a restaurant he managed. "We were friends," recalls Michelle. "We did not know that we were going to end up dating or getting married. But through my terrible experiences babysitting, I pretty much knew that parenthood was not for me. So when we began dating, it was one of the first things we talked about."

Early in his life, Naji had assumed he would become a father. "I come from a large family, and this was expected. But in my early twenties, I started thinking differently. I would tell myself that if the desire ever hit me—that instinct—that's what I was going to wait for. And it just never happened."

Both Michelle and Naji were youngest children, and when Michelle turned fourteen, she began to be recruited to baby-sit. "I didn't like kids at all," she admits. "I had one particular horrific experience with two boys, still in diapers, and it was just a nightmare. And I thought, *I can't do that ever again.* And then my sister had a child. I did like my nephew, but I liked handing him back over to her, too. I just couldn't imagine doing that every single day."

Although when they got engaged, both Michelle and Naji were 100 percent onboard with not having kids, they acknowledged there was a chance things might change. Michelle said she anticipated "some type of hormonal combustion," and Naji "had a feeling Michelle was going to change her mind." So they made a plan.

According to Naji, it went like this: "We'll get married, and then we'll talk about it if you wake up one morning and say, 'I've got to have a baby.' We'll wait until you're thirty and make a final decision then. Actually, we ended up waiting two more years, until Michelle was thirty-two."

Michelle did say that she believed in the idea of a maternal instinct. Shortly after I interviewed her, she started her own business. Ironically, she was hiring herself out as a sitter—but this time the babies were other people's pets. "People tell me, 'I think you'd make a great parent because of the way you treat your dogs.' But my dogs aren't kids. I probably have that maternal instinct—it's just that I don't want to act on it."

"I'm a little different from Michelle," Naji interjects. "I've always liked kids. At one point in my family, there were thirteen children between the ages of six and sixteen. Twelve were boys. These are nephews and young cousins I've basically helped raise."

Naji speculated about whether his friends were having kids because they really wanted them or because of peer pressure— "because 'hey, this other couple's had kids. It's the greatest thing. Let's do it. . . . ' My friends have turned out to be good parents, but I don't think all of them were really looking inside. They were just doing it because their friends had kids."

Both Michelle and Naji felt desire should be a prerequisite for parenthood, but Michelle thought people should go the extra mile and test their preparedness before having a child.

"I remember that old *Frasier* episode where Niles was trying to decide if he wanted to have a baby, so he carried around a five-pound bag of flour. And all these things happened to it: He scorched it near the fireplace; he left it in the rain. I think sometimes people should do that, or at least own a pet before they have a child."

I thought back to Michelle's "horrific" baby-sitting experiences and asked her how she responded when people say, "Oh, it's so different when they're yours."

"I just don't know what to say." Michelle had stopped going to baby showers because "it's a traumatic experience," made so by the suggestion that she was making a grave mistake by remaining childless. "I mean, I'm very happy for my friend who's having the baby, and I'll play all the games. But everybody there usually has children, and they gang up on me, saying things like 'Oh, you'd be a great parent—and it would be wonderful.'"

Michelle has felt the isolation that comes with making the alternate choice. In her circle of close friends and relatives, she can't think of one person who does not have a child. "You kind of lose a little bit of your friendship because of the children. So it's always tough."

"I've always had acquaintances or friends who don't have kids," said Naji. "A person who works for me is in his late fifties, and he's like me; he told me, 'I've yet to wake up and regret not having kids.'"

I asked Michelle how she responded to the question "Do you have kids?"

"A lot of times that's the opener in a conversation. I usually say, 'Yes, we have two four-legged children.' Because if you just say no, they're thinking, *Uh-oh, what are we going to talk about?* Or they're thinking maybe we can't have them, that there's a medical reason or something."

"Or that you're selfish," Naji says, bristling. "I say, 'No, I'm not selfish; it would be wrong to have kids just because you're telling me my mind will change, and then end up not being a good parent.'"

Michelle and Naji had done the exercise of imagining what parenthood would look like for them. Naji's crazy hours working at restaurants would mean that Michelle would basically be like a single, stay-at-home mom, because neither of them believed in putting a kid in daycare. "Yes, we had serious discussions about all that," said Naji.

"When Naji's mom retired from her job, she called us and said, 'I can take care of your child now, because I know you don't like daycare.'" Michelle laughed. "And I said, 'Oh, okay, we'll get to work on that right away.' I think she thought that was the primary motivation for us."

Michelle remembered enduring a lot of pressure from family members. "We went to so many christenings of nephews and nieces and cousins of his, and they'd always say, 'Next year it'll be you,' and we'd just stand there and smile."

"And it doesn't have to be a christening," Naji said. "It's any kind of celebration. There's a saying in Arabic that means, 'God's will, this time next year you'll have a baby.'"

Michelle's parents knew there was only a slim possibility that Michelle would end up having a baby, and Michelle recalled how they hoped the arrival of her sister's child would change her mind. "He was a pretty good child, easy to get along with. And I think they thought he might turn me—but he didn't."

Like others I had interviewed, Michelle had also come to the conclusion that there are too many unwanted children in the world. She had a hard time reconciling that belief with the Catholic tradition in which she was raised, "where you have got to procreate right away." However, Michelle and Naji were married in Naji's church, which is Eastern Orthodox Christian, and she was comforted by the words of Naji's priest, who told them, "You'll know when it's your time to have children."

Naji had had conversations with customers at the restaurants he's managed—"people who don't know me from Adam," he clarified—"and they're surprised I've been married this long with no children. And they'll say things like 'Well, God says that you have to have children.' And I'm saying, 'No, God would have put the desire in me.' On the other side, you talk to some people about your reasons, and you can just see in their face that they have regrets about having kids—their facial expression gives it away."

Naji managed family-style restaurants, so he was accustomed to the questions, the kids running around, and the chaos and noise those circumstances bring about. On the nights they had together, Michelle preferred to dine in quiet places where there were few kids. "He has the ability to block it out quite a bit; I don't have that ability." They also enjoyed traveling, staying at bed-and-breakfasts, and hiking.

"Sometimes we run into other people who don't have children, which is always nice," said Michelle. Naji admitted, "We drifted apart from our long-term friends who have children," but that was really the only downside they could think of when I asked about the disadvantages of remaining childfree. Michelle added, "I've also had people ask me, 'Well, what are you going to do when you get old?' I've never given that too much thought. I guess we'll go into a retirement center."

"And my answer's always been 'Well, we've got plenty of nephews and nieces to take care of us,'" said Naji. "A brother of mine has six kids."

Michelle and Naji were among the first couples I interviewed, and I expected to find more people like Michelle who didn't particularly like kids. However, I ended up meeting many more people like Naji, who felt very comfortable around

kids but had chosen not to have them for other, equally compelling reasons—such as a lack of desire.

DIANE AND NICK

From the moment I met Diane and Nick, I could tell they loved
sharing the same space. They even shared some physical char-
acteristics—dark hair, wide smiles—though Nick was of Italian and English descent and Diane's background was Mexican
and Native American, from a maternal line that went back to
Geronimo. Both in their early forties, they seemed too young
to have been married seventeen years.

Diane was the youngest of seven children, and Nick was
an only child. They met when Diane's nephew threw a party
and reintroduced his aunt to his best friend, Nick. They'd been
together ever since.

Nick remembered a time in his teens when he said, "I'm
never getting married. I'm never having kids"—he'd just never
imagined himself as a dad. "I was very independent, being an
only child. I didn't want to be tied down to being a parent."

Diane knew from her experiences caring for younger family members that motherhood was "really not for me," she said.
"My niece, who's three years younger than me, had a child
who Nick and I would take care of—so for a while there we
practically had a child of our own."

Nick was grateful that he and Diane were "on the same
page" on the issue of kids. "We really felt like this was one of
those situations where God led us to be together. But over the
years, we have occasionally asked each other, 'Are you sure?'"

Diane remembered days when she would "get that little
maternal instinct going" and say to Nick, "Oh, come on, I think
we should have one." But the feeling didn't last long, because
there was a handy cure. "One of our close friends was a daycare
provider, and we'd go over there and help her out, and—"

"One day of that," Nick interjected, "and she'd say, 'Okay, that's right, that's why I don't have kids.' God bless them—they're beautiful and fun—but we were just so exasperated."

I asked if their parents had given them any advice on the subject of parenthood.

Nick piped up first. "The only thing I've ever gotten from my mom is 'When are you going to have a kid? You need to have children. The family name is going to die if you're the only boy.'"

Diane said that her mother took it in stride. "I told her, 'We chose not to have children, Mom.' And she just said, 'That's okay, that's okay.' It didn't matter to her, as long as I was happy."

"We took a lot of pressure from Aunt Stella, though," said Nick, remembering the times when Diane's aunt had brought out a photo of the grandkids and asked, "When? What is wrong with you?"

Aunt Stella was old-school Catholic, and while Nick was raised in the Catholic faith as well, as an adult he chose to attend a multidenominational Christian church because he didn't "jive with the whole Catholic philosophy." Nick admitted to feeling "a little bit" guilty about the fact that "God wants us to multiply" and he was opting out, but, he said, "We felt like when we had to take care of her mom and dad, this was the trade-off."

Diane explained, "When we got together, I told Nick there was going to be a point in our lives, or in my life, when I would have to care for my parents. So there was a time—a good, solid six years of caring for them—when the good Lord said, 'All right, you're going to be selfish and not have kids—*bam!* There you go.'"

"And it was like having children," said Nick. "Their health was at a stage where they needed constant care. The rest of the family wanted to pitch in, but they were busy with their kids, so we moved them in with us. We learned a lot about caregiving. It was a very spiritual, beautiful, labor-of-love thing. But it was just like raising eighty-year-old kids; instead of a stroller, you've got a wheelchair—but you've still got diapers involved. I just can't imagine having had to raise children alongside that. I mean, I have to take my hat off to the people who do have a lot of kids."

"I look at my girlfriend with her three boys," said Diane. "She has a million-dollar business, and she does this with her boys. I guess they call it multitasking. . . . "

"They call it 'no sleep,' is what they call it," Nick quipped.

"So what do you say to those people who tell you that you can't find fulfillment unless you have a child?" I asked.

"Well, that's what our friends have told us," said Nick. "You have to do it or your life isn't going to feel complete. I don't understand why, though; it's a foreign concept to me. I feel fulfilled because I feel connected with everybody. Our whole thing is to help other people; we help our family as much as we possibly can."

Nick and Diane had recently handled the funeral arrangements for Diane's aunt, who was childless. "We were kind of like her kids," explained Nick. They told me about how they'd flown back to Denver and made sure everything was taken care of for her.

"My aunt could not have children," Diane said, "and she told us it's a very, very lonely life. And that kind of scares me now and again. But I've got nieces and nephews. . . . "

I asked them how they felt now. "Do you feel isolated, or do you have friends who are childless?" I asked.

"Well, now we really don't," said Nick. "We don't socialize that much, because when we were caring for her mom and dad those six years, we didn't have a social life. It's only been a year since her mom passed away, and we don't go out to bars or clubs or anything."

"We've always liked it that way, though," said Diane. "It's always been us. We do everything together."

Nick agreed. "We're like the same person. There's no boys' night out or girls' night out. It's like, why? I've got my best friend—why would I leave her at home to go out with the guys? Life's short—that's why we're trying to enjoy it together as much as we possibly can, just drink in everything."

Diane added that she'd learned a great deal by being a primary caregiver for her parents until their passing. "Everything is so material, but you can't take it with you in the end. So it's like, be happy. People make life so hard for themselves. And they play out that hardness. But you don't have to make it hard on yourself. Life is hard enough."

LILI AND MARIO

When Mario contacted me, offering to share his story, I was excited because he lived in Mexico. I knew from my research that the childless by choice have a harder time navigating in communities that are family-centric, and Mexico, with its strong cultural emphasis on family and faith, is much more that way than either the United States or Canada.

Mario and his wife, Lili, were comfortable communicating in English by email, so we conducted the interview that way. I sent them each a list of questions from my menu, as well as more specific questions later to clarify their responses.

At the time we corresponded, Mario was forty years old and Lili was thirty-six. Mario was a busy entrepreneur who loved juggling his multiple businesses. Lili was a law school graduate working toward a degree in psychotherapy. They had been married five years, together for seven.

Mario had previously enjoyed a bachelor's lifestyle. He had dated women with children but had never been tempted to have one of his own. "I imagined a life without my own children long before meeting Lili. I remember, back in my twenties, not liking babies or very young children," he wrote.

"As I was growing up, my parents passed on—unconsciously, I'm sure—the message of how difficult life was raising me and my sister: how many sacrifices they made, and how they constantly struggled to give us a better life.

"When my cousins and friends became parents, I listened to them complain about how difficult it was for them to pay school expenses and how they felt tied to jobs they do not like, to get money to pay for their children's needs. I realized how different and pleasant life could be without the responsibilities and restrictions that a child poses. I do not remember consciously deciding not to have children, but I recall not wanting them and being not interested in women who wanted them."

Mario's preferences became problematic for him because Lili, the woman he had fallen in love with and wanted to marry, did want children. Mario came to realize that if he wanted this special relationship to last, he might have to compromise.

"Lili eagerly wanted to have a child," he wrote. "In my opinion, a great deal of her desire came from social pressure. Despite the fact that I did not want to become a parent, I thought that one child would not be so bad—mostly because we agreed that she would take on most of the child-rearing tasks. I wanted to stay with Lili, and saw this compromise as my ticket to continue with her."

I asked Lili if she thought there was such a thing as maternal instinct, and she replied, "Yes, I think there is, but maybe this instinct gets bigger because of the culture and values that you grow up with." In her teens and early twenties, Lili fully expected to be a parent, but what she envisioned was "something very curious. I never imagined myself pregnant. Instead I imagined myself marrying somebody who already had children, or adopting one. The idea of getting pregnant scared me."

Lili talked about her own upbringing and the expectation to have children. "In my family it was taken for granted that I would have children," she said. "My mother has ten siblings, and they all have children. All my cousins my age or older have children; I just thought that after my marriage I would have babies, like it was something automatic."

It turned out not to be.

Lili recalled a time she referred to as the "pregnancy seeking crisis," a period shortly after her marriage when she and Mario tried to conceive. "I felt excited and hopeful. I imagined how my baby would look—her voice, her drawings. I even chose a name. I felt obsessive for a baby. It seemed that only pregnant women were popping up into my sight; the only TV commercials I saw were baby-related; I paid attention only to how many women in my social circles were moms. I felt excluded.

"Sometimes I felt pregnancy symptoms, and when my period came, I felt devastated. I began to blame myself for having something bad in my body, because in my family it was always said that the women were especially fertile." Like many who actively try to conceive, Lili began to perceive babymaking as a chore. "After two years, I began to feel intercourse was like an obligation instead of a pleasure and a love act, and problems with Mario came up."

Mario agreed. "I stopped enjoying sex and tried to distract myself by working, reading, or playing video games instead. Then I came to feel frustrated because the woman I once found very sexy and interesting came to be dull and only focused on an objective that for me was not a priority at all."

Mario then explained how the pregnancy seeking became a crisis. "After more than a year, pregnancy was not achieved. Lili was very sad and disappointed. I was indifferent, but I felt sad for her, so we went to specialists and found that infertility treatments were tremendously time-consuming, painful, stressful, and demanding. I began to fear that Lili would want to go through all the fertility treatment stuff. I did not. Adoption was not for me, either, and yet I did not want to be an obstacle in her quest for a child. I realized there were only two ways to go: to remain childfree together or to end our marriage. The decision would be hers."

"I imagined my life without him," said Lili, "and I felt so sad. Then I came to be conscious of what my priorities were, and I decided to continue my life with Mario. I realized that I would be happier staying with him."

Mario said that he went through a lot of sleepless nights preparing himself in case Lili decided that she needed to leave. Mario "felt an intense relief" when Lili told him of her decision to stay with him and remain childfree. However, he worried that she was just accepting it, and that many challenges still lay ahead for them.

Mario found out that extending an invitation to Lili to be part of his less child-centric world would be the key to their continued success together. "I have been inviting her to a lot of activities that I enjoy and are not related to children. We enjoy spending time with a few childfree friends we have met on the way, and with people who, despite having children, have a wider world and not child-centered lives."

When I asked Lili, "What do you do with your time together?" she responded that the question should be "What do you *not* do together?" She ticked off a list that included going to the theater, concerts, and antique-car exhibitions, playing with their nieces, traveling, and talking over coffee or a good meal.

While Mario talked about a couple he had met earlier in his life who had served as childfree role models, Lili had few such mentors. "I have some bad days when I wake up with a strong desire to be a mother, but thinking back to the pregnancy seeking crisis takes that desire away. Maybe having children would have given more happiness to us, but I am not sure at this point. I am beginning to learn to live with this idea. I think it is more important for me to have this special and beautiful marriage."

I asked her what her family thought about her choice. "I do not have problems with my parents or my brothers," she replied. "It's my cousins and other relatives. They feel sorry for me—poor, infertile girl! One aunt gave me a religious portrait and told me she would pray for me. Some friends advise me on adoption or fertility treatments without caring to ask if I am looking for a baby or have decided to stay childfree."

Lili still gets rude and intrusive questions from women now and again, but now she comes prepared: "If they ask, 'Why do you not have children?' I answer, 'Because I don't,' and I turn the conversation to them, saying, 'Tell me about yourself.' Another good answer I give is 'I have a boy.' And when they ask, 'How old?' I bounce back and respond, 'He is forty and loves cartoons!' Then the other women begin to talk about their husbands or partners."

When asked about the assumptions people make, Mario said, "The most unfair, I think, is that we are selfish. Furthermore, in Mexican culture, motherhood is almost a veneration and fatherhood is a must to be considered an adult, so people will not easily accept the childfree status as truth. Instead, they will assume there is a fertility problem, or that you are a freaky child hater."

So what is their childfree life like? When prompted to describe their marriage, Lili responded, "It's fabulous! Full of love, laughter, spontaneity, and respect. Every day with my husband is a great day!"

Mario appreciates the time he has with Lili, and the "time to build my business and take more risks. Not devoting time to a child keeps stress out of me."

Lili, too, values a less stressful life. "Since the moment I made the decision, I have felt more relaxed; it is like my internal voice says to me, *Yes, it was a good choice!*"

I asked Mario what he thought his life would look like when he got older. "I imagine myself practicing sports, writing books, teaching and coaching employees or younger people, and still being active in positions—like president or honorary president in my companies. I see myself enjoying the sense of achievement and all the material and nonmaterial rewards from it. Maybe becoming the supercool part-time grandfather if my favorite niece decides to have kids."

Mario and Lili valued the presence of children in their lives and recognized their value as mentors, or aunty and uncle, in a child's life. They were asserting their ideals and creating new pathways in a country where parenthood remains a compelling and powerful assumption.

I suspect Mario felt more empowered to resist the combination of cultural, family, and peer pressure to have kids because he could, his desire and his will buttressed by a belief he expressed in one of his first emails to me: "Parenthood is a choice, not an obligation. We are not against the parenting decision; we respect parents, and so we want to be respected."

Lili, who had clearly struggled with her decision, was beyond caring what people thought and had learned to value the gift of autonomy: "I have a formula for happiness: Look for it inside myself, live right here and right now, and focus on what I have, not what I have not."

Some might argue that Lili represents the gray area between childless by circumstance and childless by choice. I contend that she is childless by choice by virtue of the fact that she identifies herself as such, and because she chooses consciously and freely to remain in her marriage with Mario, even though she knew that by doing so, she would most likely remain childless. Her situation is not unusual; I met others who had a miscarriage or tried to conceive for a time, then made a conscious choice not to continue trying to have a child or to pursue fertility treatments or adoption.

Lili and Mario's story is an example of the acquiescer's process and represents the challenges of deciding to remain childless in a culture that does not provide many childfree role models. Mario and Lili show us the importance of owning our choices and defining happiness for ourselves as we forge a sense of well-being in the midst of occasional self-doubt.

TAMARA AND JASON

Tamara emailed me about participating in this project, and when I replied I asked her, as I did all my subjects, if her husband of five years would agree to be interviewed, too. She responded, "I will talk to him after the drugs wear off." She was having a hysterectomy the next day.

For most thirty-five-year-old childless women, a hysterectomy would have been a sad occasion, but not for Tamara, who told me, "I knew since I was eleven years old that I was childfree." Her husband, Jason, who was a couple of years younger, also wanted to remain childless; however, he'd never thought he would have that choice—until he proposed to Tamara.

Their story was full of surprises. When I asked my first question—"How did you meet?"—Tamara replied, "I don't remember." How could she? They were toddlers.

"His mother and my stepmother went to nursing school together, so he was part of my peer group at my dad's house," Tamara said. "Then we didn't see each other for twelve years. We bumped into each other again at my brother's wedding and I thought, *Oh, he grew up nice.* It was almost like we were waiting for each other, and we got married less than a year later.

"Ten minutes after he asked me to marry him, I said, 'I don't want to have kids.' And—I'll never forget this—he sighed with relief and said, 'I thought I was going to have to have kids or not get married.'"

"I never wanted to have kids," Jason said, "but I had resigned myself to it, because every woman I ever dated wanted children. I don't know that it ever occurred to me that there were other options until I got into my mid-twenties."

Tamara had come to that realization much earlier in life. "I was one of those children who couldn't be fed the line 'You get married and have kids.' I am the product of a teenage pregnancy and a marriage that lasted a very short time. Friends of my parents were having 'oops' pregnancies or having children singly, so I saw [parenthood] as something separate from getting married. The moment I remember knowing I didn't want kids was when I got my period. The cramps were horrible, and I was talking to someone about it—I think it was my dad—and he said, 'Now you can have kids.' And I'm thinking, *I'm eleven—why am I even thinking about having kids?* And I said, 'I don't want this.' His response was 'Well, you don't have a choice. It's what you do when you grow up. You're not grown up until you have them.'"

You can imagine how that went over. "One of the worst things you can do is tell me I have to do something," Tamara confirmed. "It was ridiculous. My mom did the right thing. She was like, 'This happened to me—let's talk about this so it won't happen to you.' She has always been very supportive of my decision not to have kids. My mother has a great-aunt who turned down marriage proposals in the '50s. She never got married and never had kids, and I have an uncle who never had kids. So I had a bunch of childfree role models growing up."

Jason, on the other hand, did not. Regarding his family, he said, "Um, let's just say they are less than understanding. I'm the oldest of the grandchildren. My brother finally had a baby girl in February, so my mother has her grandchild now, and that gets the pressure off me. But it was hard on my family because I think they assumed I wanted to have kids, and when they found out we weren't going to, I don't think they believed it."

"My hysterectomy helped," said Tamara, laughing. Remaining childfree was not the primary impetus for the surgery, however—she had adenoids in her uterus, an extremely painful condition. "I really needed this hysterectomy, and our childfree status helped the doctor feel okay about it. Jason had a vasectomy six months after we got married. Other than his brother, we never told his side of the family. My surgeon talked about other therapy but said, 'The way we do hysterectomies today, it's going to be less invasive than anything else we could do. Are you sure you don't want to have kids?' I was able to say, 'Yes, absolutely,' using Jason's vasectomy as proof. That saved me a year of getting biopsies and getting pecked and chipped away at. When I had the surgery and the biopsy, they told me that a hysterectomy would have been the only thing that would have worked anyway.'"

The three of us talked about how difficult it can be for childfree people to get a procedure that renders them sterile. Tamara was frustrated by her efforts to find a doctor who would give Jason a vasectomy: "It makes me mad. We had to make several calls; some of them said that we needed to go to counseling. Some of the things they suggested were really spooky, like write a letter to the child you'll never have."

When they finally found a doctor, Jason said, "he didn't try to talk us out if it, but he did make us convince him. I was only twenty-eight at the time."

"What offended me is that, as the patient's wife, I had to sign a release form," said Tamara. "I'm like, 'Excuse me—it's his body!'"

The doctor's precautions pointed to the societal assumption that people, especially young people, will change their minds and want to have kids later in life. Yet, as Tamara explained to Jason's doctor, "If we ever changed our minds, I would have no problem adopting. I have a lot of steps and halves in my family; my family doesn't have to come from my body."

But even within her fragmented family, there were subtle pressures to have biological children. "I was raised by my mother's second husband, who is black. So there's that African American thing that you have kids. That's very strong in the culture. Although there are members of his family who have come to accept our choice, they don't understand it."

Jason saw similar responses play out in his everyday interactions with people. "You'll be talking about being married, and it's always 'Do you have kids yet?' People think that if you don't have them, it's just a matter of time," he said. He felt as if the reaction to his and Tamara's decision not to have kids was often either surprise or disapproval.

"It's like you have to prove you're not a child hater," said Tamara. "A woman at work came in with her child, and she needed to have an impromptu meeting. So I said, 'Give her to me and we'll walk around,' and so we did. I like this kid and she likes me, but this guy walks up to me and says, 'I thought you didn't like kids'—like he was accusing me."

Tamara and Jason were very comfortable around kids and had cared for younger siblings and cousins. "The only thing I didn't do was breastfeed or give birth," said Tamara. "Sometimes people will be talking about their kids and I'll chime in with a story about my little brother, and they just look at me like I have three heads. The reactions span from 'Oh, I can't believe you have experienced that!' to 'How can you experience that and still not want a kid?'"

So if these two were not childfree because they didn't like kids, then why were they?

"There are many reasons," Jason said. He alluded to their combined families' history of severe medical problems which included cancer, depression, diabetes, and heart disease. However, his main motive was more to the point: "I enjoy our life the way it is. I don't feel the need to introduce something that requires that much more responsibility, cost, and work on top of everything else I already have. And it's not something I want, and that's really the bottom line."

Tamara also talked about her family history. "Every woman on my mother's side of the family has had clinical depression, and I'm going to pass that on?" Beyond genetics, she cited environmental reasons, too: "There are three billion more people on Earth than is environmentally safe. Children are not a necessity in life."

Tamara felt that her domestic situation was ideal: "We do feel like a family; we *are* a family. My theory is, the reason there is so much divorce in the world is people don't consider their spouse their family."

Jason added, "We have the cats."

I had to ask, "Are pets kid substitutes?"

"No, absolutely not," said Tamara, "because if so, people with kids wouldn't have pets." This begged the question whether a maternal or paternal instinct exists. "We all have a caring instinct," Tamara said. "I don't feel the need to label it as maternal or paternal instinct, although we do call ourselves Mommy and Daddy to the cats."

Jason thought it was more than that. "I think it is genetic. I'm a scientist. Species are made to procreate, to propagate the species, and human beings are no different. The main difference is that human beings have a choice. I think the instinct is there, but people have it to different degrees or are able to suppress it."

Although Jason was on the nature side of the nature-versus-nurture debate, when I asked, "When you imagined yourself as a parent, what did you imagine it would be like?" he responded, "The only thing I ever thought of was that I would be a better father than my own. My parents divorced when I was five. Our father lived fifteen minutes away, but we hardly ever saw him until we got into our teenage years. So I never had a solid image in my mind of what it would be like to be a father."

When I read this part of the transcript later, I felt sad for Jason and other kids who did not have positive paternal role models, and I wondered to what degree the lack thereof influences these individuals' decisions. Yet when I asked Jason and Tamara if they ever regretted or perceived any downsides to their decision to remain childfree, the only one they could think of was having to deal with other people's perceptions of them.

Tamara felt she had everything she needed. "We're best friends, and that's something I've always wanted. I'm bisexual, so I could have ended up with a woman, but whoever I ended up with had to like me and want to spend time with me, as well as love me."

"We've seen a lot of bad relationships because of our family situations," said Jason. "My dad's on his third marriage. And Tamara's right—we are such good friends, and that's the most important thing for us."

"We have a very low-maintenance relationship," said Tamara. "We don't do stupid things; everything that's stereotypically stupidly female, I don't do, and everything that's stereotypically stupidly male, he doesn't do. I'm not a shopper. He remembers every birthday and anniversary, and I don't care if he does or not. I have a real temper, but it's never directed at him. I can tell when he's really upset about something—he just kind of shuts in—and I leave him alone. We see each other as people, rather than as a man or a woman."

When I asked them what their priorities were now, Jason said, "Being happy and healthy. Everybody should be that way. We set ourselves up to be that way as much as we can, and for me, having a child would really upset that balance. A good friend of mine believes that we're crazy not to have kids, because we would be such good parents and we would raise the child to be a productive and beneficial member of society. That's making a lot of assumptions, though. There are a lot of things that are not under your control, and we can help our society in other ways."

Tamara said, "I like the thought that we might be good childfree role models and never even know about it. We're not trying to convert anyone, but if they are naturally child-free, we'll be the ones they look to and say, 'Look, they're not freaks, they're not crazy.'"

LAURA AND DAN

I found Laura and Dan through the No Kidding! club in their hometown of Las Vegas. They had recently been featured in a local newspaper article about childfree couples.

As a young woman, Laura never expected she would end up in a childfree marriage. Childfree, yes, but not married: "It just seems sort of innate with me. Since I was a little girl, I pretty much felt like I didn't have a maternal instinct, just no desire to be a mother. When I met Dan, I was at a point where I didn't want to get married—ever—simply because I didn't want to have children."

Dan had begun to suspect in his teens that kids were not in his future. "It's kind of funny—I was in church, and I was already questioning being there, and then, right on cue, kids would start screaming. So I was already thinking, *I don't want anything to do with religion, and I don't want kids, either.*

"I would never think about having a child until my parents would say, 'One day when you have kids,'" Dan continued, shaking his head, unable to imagine it. "It just seemed like a really alien concept to me. And now I see the trouble people have with their kids, and I see other people who have good kids, and it seems like this roulette wheel that you're betting on. I've never been one to shirk responsibility; I have a lot of responsibility now. It's just that that kind of responsibility has never been attractive to me."

Yet he was happy to marry—Dan and Laura were in their early thirties at the time of our interview, but they had been together fourteen years and married for eleven. I was curious about Laura—a person who didn't want to get married because she didn't want kids—meeting someone like Dan. I asked her, "So how did that feel, to meet a guy who doesn't care if he has children?"

"I felt like it was almost a miracle," said Laura. "I couldn't believe I was meeting somebody who had the same philosophy, goals, desires, and perspective on life as I did. We were on the same page. It seemed too good to be true." And how did Dan feel? "I got pretty lucky," he concurs.

I went back to Laura's comment about always knowing she didn't have "a maternal instinct."

"Obviously," I said, "you believe there is such a thing."

"Yes, I do, and I believe that it's very possible that people who have no maternal instinct have children anyway. Which, I think, is not very good for children."

Laura was convinced she was hardwired not to have kids. "A lot of people who are gay feel like they were born gay. I feel like I was born with a lack of a maternal instinct."

Laura recalled being a preschooler and feeling pressured to "play Mommy" with her peers. "That's what all the other little girls did, so I tried to force myself to play Mommy. It felt so unnatural, even then. I thought to myself, *This isn't right. I don't want to be a mommy when I grow up.* That was my first 'aha' moment—if in your gut it doesn't feel right, then it's not right."

Dan said, "I have cousins whose paternal instinct doesn't always show, but when it does, it's like, *Ah, that's why you had a kid.*"

"We don't hate children," said Laura, "we just don't have a whole lot of patience for children, to be honest."

Dan worked out of his home as a writer, and he struggled to imagine what his life would be like with children: "being interrupted to blow someone's nose or clean someone's mess, or trying to be oblivious in my office when there's chaos going on out in the living room. How do I explain to a two-year-old why I'm neglecting him? I think I have come to the conclusion that I would probably be more neglectful than I would want to be as a parent, just because of the things that I want to pursue in life."

"What, if anything, did your parents tell you about parenting?" I asked them, turning back to a question I ask all my interview subjects.

Laura answered first. "My parents always made it seem like it was really difficult. The reason my parents got married was because my mother got pregnant with my sister. Mom's all of nineteen years old; my dad is maybe twenty-two, in college. And later they were very frank with me—the reason they had me was because they were on the verge of breaking up and I was going to save their marriage. They got divorced nine years later, so obviously it didn't work."

"Hmmm," Dan said, trying to be delicate. "Well, I don't want to say who said it, but I often heard that being a parent was hard, and I often got a laundry list of things that were being done for me that I didn't appreciate well enough, apparently. My parents divorced when I was in college, and maybe that affected whether or not I wanted to have kids. I don't know; I haven't examined it too much."

Although they were both children of divorce, Dan and Laura's marriage appeared solid. They had even recently renewed their vows at an "Elvis wedding," joined by friends and family.

I asked Dan to describe their relationship: "We love each other very much. We share a lot of ideals, and we're just very comfortable with each other. We met when we were nineteen, so we went into adulthood together."

"We have a really solid friendship," Laura responded. "And I think that's what gets us through. When we're acting like husband and wife—when I tend to be nagging, when he tends to be obstinate—that's usually when we butt heads. Then when we step back and we realize that we're friends, we're on the same team, and we've got the same goals, then everything takes a turn for the better."

Laura is Mexican American, and Dan is Caucasian. Both were raised Catholic but now describe themselves as "recovering Catholics" and atheists. So I was curious: "Can you be a Catholic and be childless by choice?"

"According to theology, you shouldn't be able to be, because Catholics aren't supposed to practice birth control," said Dan. "So we should've had—"

"Oodles of children," Laura intervened, laughing.

"I'm very much an idealistic purist. I believe you practice something 100 percent or you're being hypocritical," said Dan. "I think that's what became so confusing for me, one of the reasons I knew that I didn't want to continue being a Catholic. I looked at other religions and said, *Forget it.* The thing I can practice is atheism, for sure."

"And cynicism," Laura added, smiling.

Even though Laura and Dan had moved away from the Catholic Church, they still felt outside pressure to have children. But not from Laura's parents, who were "really supportive. It's more aunts, uncles, and cousins," Laura said. "One of Dan's cousins had a baby about two years ago, and it was like, 'Dan and Laura are next.'"

Dan agreed that the pressure was mostly from his side of the family. "My mom started commenting, 'Well, you know I've got to be a grandma at some point.' So I had to tell her, 'We've chosen not to have children, Mom.'"

"It's almost as though Dan and I have to hold up a sign saying we don't want to have children," Laura said. "Joining No Kidding! and being featured in the newspaper was a big part of making that statement, and now the pressure's really eased up." They had found a community of like-minded people with whom they could share the benefits and the challenges of a childfree life.

When I asked about the downsides to being childfree, Dan couldn't come up with one thing, but Laura did feel the sting of the perception of childlessness: "this idea that part of being a woman is having a child—you're not really a woman until you're a mother."

Dan considered this and agreed. "That's true, like you're somehow going to be incomplete if you don't have kids."

"Yeah, like I'm somehow shortchanging myself or I'm shortchanging Dan. The first question is 'How does your husband feel about you not wanting children?' Well, he agrees with me—otherwise I wouldn't be married to him."

"Not for very long," added Dan.

Both Dan and Laura lived by Laura's credo: "You've got to do what's best for you. You can't live your life for other people."

But isn't that selfish? Laura felt we needed to redefine what it means to be selfish, and quoted Oscar Wilde: "Selfishness is not living as one wishes to live, it is asking others to live as one wishes to live."

LISA AND TOM

Shortly after Lisa and Tom were married, they started getting emails from family asking, "How's the grandkid coming along?"

The emails were in jest, Tom said, "but with truth behind it." Of course they would have children—Lisa and Tom thought so, too. They were both in their mid-thirties, in a solid, loving relationship. Only after they got pregnant and lost the child did they begin to imagine a life without children.

"We wanted kids, but then when we thought about the possibility of not having kids, it just became so clear that, wait a minute, it's not just an assumption that you're going to have kids—or it shouldn't be," said Lisa. "It should be a very, very well-thought-out decision."

Tom remembered that they would check in with each other periodically: "Well, do you want to try now? And it was kind of like, 'Well, no, let's wait.' We were in the midst of either a move or a job change, or it just didn't feel right. And I don't think either one of us could really put our finger on what it was that was keeping us from saying, 'Yes, let's just go ahead and do it; there may never be a perfect time.'"

Lisa concurred. "We would literally sit down at the kitchen table on a monthly basis and ask, 'Okay, how do you feel?' We would sometimes even write down pros and cons. And almost every single time, the cons side had more items on it."

Tom recalls the day when "we just looked at each other and we both said, at the same time, 'Do we even want to have children?'"

It was out, finally, but for Tom and Lisa it wasn't the end of the conversation. "We still talk about it," Tom said, "just to make sure we're still on the same page, and so far we are."

Lisa said, "It's hard for us to think that people don't have that conversation."

I had to laugh, because I felt the same way when parents told me they had never had this all-important talk. Going into this project, I thought every couple had the "kid conversation." I was shocked to find so many couples who admitted they had never sat down and discussed kids until one was on the way.

"It's really sad and scary," Tom said.

Lisa didn't want to judge. "I must say that we were part of that norm, you know. Prior to even considering not having children, we assumed that we would."

I wanted to know, "How did you feel when the two of you had made the decision?"

"It was a lot of emotion," admitted Lisa, "because for me, I was kind of shocked that I was even thinking that. So I surprised myself. I also felt a little sadness, and relief, too, so it was a mixture. Then I was curious—I was like, *hmmm.*"

"And it really was that way with both of us," said Tom. "I was thinking, *Okay, well, if we do have children, I really don't know how I'm going to feel about it.* I was becoming less and less convinced that any time was going to be a good time. It's such a huge decision to make—probably the biggest you'll ever have to make—so when we were both in agreement to not have kids, it was a tremendous relief—as well as a lot of pressure off."

Lisa tried to imagine what it would have been like had they not agreed. "What compromise do you make? It's not just a compromise—one person's going to have to give in."

"And the potential for resentment is huge," said Tom.

How had their parents reacted to the news that Tom and Lisa would remain childless? "My parents didn't take it seriously at first," said Lisa. "I think they thought that we were reacting to a situation, or that we didn't really mean it. It was just kind of like, 'They'll change their mind.'"

"I don't remember telling my parents specifically we weren't going to have children," Tom said. "But they know now, and my mother relayed something to Lisa not that long ago. . . . "

Lisa picked up the story from there. "We were at Tom's parents' house for dinner and somehow our not having kids came up, and she said something to the effect that she thought that was a really smart and good decision. It felt good to hear her say that."

This kind of support for and validation of her choice was meaningful to Lisa because she didn't experience it very often, especially since she and Tom had moved to a city in the southern United States where there were fewer openly childfree couples. I asked Lisa to describe her typical interactions with the parents in her neighborhood.

"It's definitely uncomfortable. If I know the person I'm talking with is a religious person, then I feel like they're judging me—that I'm not being a good Christian or I'm not following the Bible." Lisa, who's Jewish, saw the irony in this comment, but she understood how she might be perceived as "strange" to the women she encountered who had kids. "I used to think that about people who didn't have kids, too," she said.

Tom confessed that he'd been oblivious to Lisa's discomfort in these social situations. He told her, "I didn't know you felt that way or that you've been made to feel that way. I never have. Maybe that's just a difference between a man and a woman."

Tom did feel the social isolation, however. "We just moved into a new house. I'm out raking leaves, and our next-door neighbors are out there with their toddler, and they're like, 'Oh, hi, we're so-and-so, and do you have any kids?' And I say no, and then the conversation ends."

Lisa tried to make sense of it. "If you're not a mother, then where do you fit into society? What do you have in common with all the other women? They don't really know what to do with you, because women are supposed to be mothers."

"I think if you had children, it would be 'Why don't y'all come over, bring your child over?' and then you'd get into that whole birthday-every-weekend thing," Tom envisioned.

Instead, weekends for Tom and Lisa were devoted to house projects or the occasional weekend out of town. "We like to go out to dinner with friends," said Lisa. "We were talking about this this morning. All of our free time can be devoted to each other and to ourselves. We have the time to check in with each other, and if there's any issue we can sit down and talk about it without distractions."

"Kids take away your focus on each other," Tom concurred. "I think what happens to a lot of people is they lose touch. They become empty-nesters and realize they don't even know the person they've been living with; the only thing they've really had in common is the child and the child's activities. And then they have to refind themselves, and I think a lot of times they find that they don't want to be with each other."

Tom's parents had divorced when he was a toddler, so he understood that relationships are fragile. "I think, as selfish as it may sound, Lisa and I have a very healthy relationship because we don't have children, and that's an aspect of our quality of life that I wouldn't want to jeopardize."

"It's more important to me to have a good relationship with Tom, and be the best person that I can be, than to have those two things suffer and try to be a parent. I don't think that I would be a good parent. I've told people that, too, because I don't think it's anything to be ashamed of."

I asked Tom and Lisa, "How would you imagine your life would look if you did have children?"

Lisa responded with a barrage of words: "Hectic, frustrated, tired, frazzled . . . uh, unhappy. I want to say 'unhappy,' but I don't know if that's really the right word—but just nervous all the time."

Tom imagined himself being disorganized. "I would feel like we were always trying to play catch-up." Tom also imagined the worst-case scenarios: "You let your child play in the street and—*boom*—they get hit, or they get abducted by some crazy in the neighborhood."

"Yeah," Lisa agreed, "paranoid about everything."

While I was reviewing the transcript of this interview, I was struck by what Lisa and Tom had *not* imagined: softball games, family picnics, graduation, and school plays—happy times with children. But this was often the case when I asked couples to imagine a life as parents—and was an example of how the cons outweighed the pros for these couples.

I wondered about the process that took Lisa and Tom from anticipating parenthood without question to a place where parenthood was a daunting, undesirable, and unlikely prospect, and how Lisa had concluded that she would be a poor candidate for motherhood. Tom gave me some clues. "We have issues—issues we bring from growing up that we have consciously chosen to work on for the rest of our lives and that we feel are not completely resolved," he explained. "And because we're not there yet, it makes us hesitate to have children and risk passing that on to them."

Tom's priority was "to be the best married couple we can be. There are a lot of people who regret their decision, or they're unhappy with the way things have worked out. You just never know, but you wish there were more happy families out there."

I chose to include Lisa and Tom's story in this chapter because it is a good example of the postponer process, in which couples start out imagining parenthood for themselves but ultimately decide to be childfree. Their story shows how the assumption of parenthood is often challenged by time, circumstance, self-awareness, and open communication between partners.

KATHRYN AND MICHAEL

My cousin Darren told me about his friends Kathryn and Michael. "You should interview them," he said. "They are definitely childless *by choice.*" Michael and Kathryn, who were thirty-three and thirty-seven respectively at the time of our interview, lived in a small condo in British Columbia—one of the most beautiful places in the world, in my opinion. Their condo looked like the "after" picture on one of the home-makeover shows. And its inhabitants were equally photogenic, snuggling into each other on the sofa as we settled in to do the interview. It was as if they shared an aura.

My first question was how long they had been together.

"We've been married just over nine years," said Kathryn. "We dated for three weeks, flew to the Caribbean, and got married barefoot on the beach."

I must have looked a little stunned, because Kathryn quickly added, "We worked out all the major issues. First date, I said to Michael, 'You want kids, I'm not the girl for you, because I never want to have children.' And he said, 'I don't really know. I never really thought about it.' I said, 'You need to go home and think about it, and then you can get back to me.' The next day he comes back and says, 'I don't really think I want to have kids.' I'm like, 'I guess there's going to be a second date.'"

Then I turned to Michael. "So, what did you think about that first date?"

"I was like, *Who's this chick?*" said Michael. "It did kind of catch me off guard because I had never put too much thought into it. Traditionally, that's what you do—you finally meet someone and you have a family. So it wasn't until the question was actually posed, front and center, that I thought, *You know what, I don't really want to; now that I think about it, yeah, I completely agree.*"

"I believe in being honest up front," said Kathryn. "There's no point in waiting ten years or ten months, when you're already involved, to start talking about this."

"All the hard questions came very early," said Michael.

"And that's how I just knew he was the one," said Kathryn. "I had been married before. I did say I would never get married again; I would never change my name again. And within three weeks of meeting Michael, I'm standing on the beach saying,

'I do.' We got all the hard questions out of the way, and everything just fell into place."

Kathryn decided early that she didn't want kids. "The earliest I can remember is probably ten or eleven. I had a stay-at-home mom who gave up her career when she had children. And I think there was a little part of her that was resentful of that. And my mom was a great mom; she was PTA, cookies, your lunch bag was on the counter, and dinner was on the table at five-thirty. But it was so *Leave It to Beaver* that, I don't know, I just wanted something else."

For Michael, although he did his share of baby-sitting for the neighbors, "there was never that moment of *hey, this is going to be cool when I'm a dad.* I just never had that natural instinct or need. It was just tradition; it was just natural progression. I never put too much thought into it."

"I was a Sunday school teacher," said Kathryn, "and I did a lot of baby-sitting. I think I got a good dose of reality that contributed to my feeling that *yeah, I don't think I want to do this full-time.* I could probably do it, but grudgingly, and I don't think that's fair to a child, to be half-there and snappy or cranky."

"I've seen Kathryn around kids, and she really is great with kids," said Michael. "But it's on her terms. Same thing for me. It's not that I don't like kids, it's just that I only like them a little bit of the time." Michael knew that he was different from some of his friends who really wanted kids, who appeared to have the parenting instinct. "Just because I don't have it doesn't mean it doesn't exist."

"I never had it," said Kathryn. "We get people bringing their new babies into the dental office where I work, and all the other girls in the office want to hold the new baby, and they're like, "Oh, isn't that cute?" And I'm looking over, thinking, *Teen pregnancy, gangs, drugs, stolen cars . . . yeah, no.*"

The state of the world was something that had strongly motivated Michael's decision as well. He'd seen much of the world, and much of it wasn't very child-friendly. He worried what it would be like for a child growing up in today's culture. "The way I see it going, I don't see it as a great place for children to grow up."

Kathryn remembered what her mother had said to her when she realized Kathryn's decision to not have kids was firm. "She actually said to me, 'If I was a young person in this day and age, I would seriously be contemplating not having children.' She said there are so many other issues that you deal with as a parent these days, compared to when she had us. She totally understood, which was good."

Michael's family had a little more difficulty wrapping their minds around his decision. "It was really tough early on. I mean, three weeks and then we got married, so they didn't even know this woman I brought home one Christmas. I had the talk with my mom: 'We're not having kids. And please respect our decision.' But my grandmother, who doesn't speak a word of English, didn't understand, so there was this ninety-year-old bubba walking around the house, going, 'Baby, baby, baby.'"

"I've had girlfriends who have had a baby and have called me crying at two in the morning," said Kathryn. "The baby's screaming in the background, and she's saying, 'What did I do? I have ruined my life.' Society expects you to have a family, and some women fall into that and they just do it. But I don't think many of them really stop to ask themselves, Is this really what I want?"

Kathryn had forced Michael to think about it on their first date, and he was grateful. He thought that the brief time he'd taken to consider whether he was motivated to tackle a responsibility as huge as parenthood had been transformative. Now, he said, "I think one of the things that really irk me is that I don't think a lot of people consider that responsibility. It's *have a kid, give it a whirl.*"

Kathryn couldn't begin to imagine their life with kids. "Travel is one of the biggest things we really enjoy, just the ability to go somewhere tomorrow—pack a bag, lock our door, and leave. We've done extended trips. Can you imagine dragging a three-year-old around Europe for six weeks? I mean, you'd lose your mind. There's no way."

Kathryn suspected that some of the backlash against the childless by choice was a bit of "jealousy that we're living a lifestyle they wish they could live, but they already have kids and there's no going back."

"We've all made choices," said Michael.

"It's true. It was our choice not to have children," Kathryn answered. She suspected that if they had chosen to have kids, she might also have been jealous of Michael, who would have continued to travel extensively for work, probably without her. "Instead," she said, "I can just throw an overnight bag in the back of the car. I can go with him. There's no compromise; there's no resentment because he's out there doing things and I'm stuck at home."

Michael is self-employed and can take big chunks of vacation time between projects, and Kathryn has a flexible schedule at the dental office. I commented that most people have to wait until they're sixty for the lifestyle this couple has. Kathryn agreed and thought that was very depressing.

She recalled a time when they were in Greece when this feeling hit home. "To get to the Acropolis in Athens, you have to walk up quite a ways to see the major structure. Well, this bus pulls up behind us, and the doors open, and there's all these elderly people, some with canes. And they stand at the bottom platform, looking up at the Acropolis because they can't walk up the steep stairs to the top. I said to Michael, 'You wait your whole life to do this—you raise a family, you put them all through school, you pay for weddings—to get to this point in your life where now you can travel, and you can't even really see what you've waited your whole life to come and see.' So Michael and I just decided that would never be us. We want to see it, hike it, swim it while we still can. And we'll be happy to sit at home when we're seventy, watching videos and playing solitaire."

"Go to the early-bird dinner. Sounds perfect for me," said Michael.

I laughed at the notion that these two relatively young adults were looking forward to the time when they would be dining on the blue-plate special and going home to a game of cards. They were planning the big trips now so that when it came time to retire, they could actually . . . retire.

Radical notion. But, of course, some people will read this and think, *What a sad and lonely way to end your days—no grandchildren at the table or to play games with.*

Michael didn't get it, though. It was enough just to have the "true love" he had with Kathryn. "I don't need to have a family to complete the bond," he said. "I've got my partner; that's all I need."

Even nine years after he said "I do" to a childfree life with Kathryn, there was nothing, he claimed, "tugging at me, asking *what am I missing?* We've always lived with no regrets," said Michael. "I could go tomorrow. I hope I don't, but if I do I know I've lived such a good life."

I believed him. Kathryn and Michael did appear to be living as if each day were their last. We spent the last half hour of our interview looking through photo albums of their travels and talking about their plans for a trip to South Africa. I was also planning a trip there later that year, because a friend of mine had done the same tour and had said, "It's one of those trips you have to do before you die."

I think Kathryn and Michael would agree.

LUCKY IN LOVE

In my early teens, I used the expression "gag me with a spoon" in response to sentiments I judged too sickly-sweet or lovey-dovey. I was a cynic then, and I still am to a certain extent, though I have softened with age. So I came to the interviews with a bit of a jaded mindset, expecting people would put on their best faces in an attempt to show how perfect their lives really were. What I found instead, however, was a genuine affinity among these couples and, more often than not, a desire to respond honestly to questions that I'd designed to expose their real motives and to determine their degree of regret, agreement and disagreement, and well-being.

I expected to find self-doubt and shaky marriages. What I discovered instead were forward-looking people who were happy to lie in the bed they had made, with the partner (and often the pets) they had chosen to share their life with. They were prepared to accommodate the occasional self-doubt or negative consequences that come with the territory.

I also saw a willingness to see the silver lining in a life that others perceived as lonely, tragic, or developmentally stunted, and to suffer the downsides, whatever they might be, in exchange for the luxury of self-determination and for freedom from expectations that my interviewees deemed incongruent with their true nature.

It sometimes seemed, as Laura said, "too good to be true." Was it possible that I was only seeing the happy ones? Were the people who self-selected for interviews the type who were bound to be happy, or to show me a happy face? Were the unhappy couples hidden from me, afraid to step forward and admit publicly that they'd made a mistake? Perhaps. As in the population at large, I suspect that there are both satisfied and dissatisfied childless by choice couples. But I believe, based on my own research and that of others, that the findings of marital satisfaction and connectedness between voluntarily childless partners are valid and can be attributed, at least in part, to the fact that these couples are on the same page when it comes to their values, ideals, and priorities. Perhaps the decision-making process itself—a process that demands honest communication, agreement, and support between partners—provides a means for couples to feel understood, respected, and validated. Or maybe it comes down to just plain luck.

In *Beyond Motherhood: Choosing a Life Without Children,* Jeanne Safer wrote, "A number of women . . . told me that they thought of their husbands as their symbiotic soul mates, their 'best friends,' even as their 'twins.' These couples tend to be mutually admiring and sense that they have something rare." Safer noted that this observation was true even of couples who spent much of their time apart, and she thought there was more to it than just pure luck—"since [these] couples have chosen to focus their intimate lives solely on each other, they gravitate to relationships that facilitate the particular combination of independence and mutuality that they crave."[1]

I also noted this pattern, particularly in the case of early articulators: Not only did these individuals choose a life without kids, but they also consciously chose spouses they thought they could enjoy as intimate lifetime partners—in a family of two. As Laura said about Dan, "We don't just love each other— I also really, really like him." Is the bar of compatibility, or affinity, set higher because these couples know there will be no distractions in the form of children, no reason to stay together if they become unhappy?

As I sat at my computer, pondering this question, my mantra surfaced: *Happiness is a choice.* It is not something that is bestowed upon you, or happens only to those who are deserving or lucky, or who have kids or don't have kids. And if my mantra is true, is that what these couples were doing— choosing happiness? Or is it that the freedom to choose brings happiness?

What I do know from my interviews with childless by choice couples is that these partnerships are valid and filled with enough friendship, love, and mutual respect to sustain these couples over many years of marriage. It is also true that, as a nonvisible minority, these couples are fortunate to have found each other, and to have remained in agreement about what is likely one of the most important decisions of their lives.

CHAPTER 6

Marginal and Misunderstood:
The Myths and Realities of Living Childfree

"That's selfish." I was in a friend's kitchen, discussing the common motives for remaining childfree, including my own, when she made this rebuke. I was stung. Here was a person who knew me and liked me, so I thought. But apparently she saw a serious flaw. I didn't want to be a parent, so I had pursued other interests, like work, travel, and volunteering with youth. My childless status freed me to make these alternate choices, but in her judgment they were motivated primarily by selfishness. In that moment, I wondered what, short of working with lepers in the slums of Calcutta, could redeem my intentionally childless soul.

Later, I invited attendees of the 2005 No Kidding! Convention in Philadelphia to share with me "the dumbest question you have ever been asked as a childfree person." One woman recalled the time a coworker, informed of her childfree status, asked incredulously, "You and your husband don't have kids?! *So what do you do?*"

There are five definitions, or senses, of the word "marginal" in my *Webster's New Collegiate Dictionary,* two of which seem to accurately describe my experience being childless by choice in North America:

1. Located at the fringe of consciousness.
2. Close to the lower limit of qualification, acceptability, or function.[1]

If you can't imagine a life without kids or you believe parenthood is the only responsible pathway to maturity and fulfillment, or that all married couples should have children in order to propagate the species, preserve our way of life, or serve God's will, how might you respond to the intentionally childless couple?

Judgmentally or supportively? Or perhaps you'd rather not think about it at all, because doing so might open up this prickly question: Why *do* we have kids?

Perhaps it's just easier to cling to the idea that the childless by choice are a minority of nutcases who are in a hopeless state of arrested development, crippled by infantile needs and selfish desires.

THE SELFISH ASSUMPTION AND OTHER MYTHICAL MONSTERS

After that evening with my friend, I felt compelled to define "selfish" for myself. What did it mean to me? I understood it to represent people who pursue their own needs or wants without regard for others. I certainly identified with the first part of the definition—I *was* focused on my own needs and desires. I was an entrepreneur who lived by the credo "Do what you love, and success will follow." I believed firmly in the win-win principle—that looking after your own best interests and the interests of others are not mutually exclusive pursuits. I happily gave to charities, volunteered my time mentoring teens, and paid taxes. So I felt that the second part of the definition—"without regard for others"—didn't apply to my situation. The negative connotations of selfishness involve the selfish person victimizing someone. Whom was I hurting? Other than depriving my parents of a grandchild, I felt fairly certain that my "selfish" path had been free of roadkill.

Call me self-determining, not selfish.

The "selfish" label should not have bothered me. If I know I'm not selfish, why should I care what other people think? But I did. And I do—for myself and the other childfree by choice. If we allow these stereotypes to persist or go unchallenged, we invite discrimination and marginalization. If others believe we have chosen the childfree path based purely on selfish motives, then they can assume selfishness trumps all the other, more compelling reasons to remain childless.

When I started my research, I quickly found that I was not the only childfree person disturbed by the "selfish" label. When I asked my participants, "What myth or assumption about people who are childfree/childless by choice do you feel is the most unfair or misleading?" the response I received most often was: "that we are selfish."

One of my participants, Kathryn, said, "I think that thinking it through and deciding not to bring a child into this world—knowing the type of person you are—is one of the most unselfish acts you can do."

Kathryn knew women who had remarried who already had children from a previous marriage, and yet had felt pressured by their new husband to have another child, due to what Kathryn characterized as ego. "He wants to have his own child, to carry on his name; the stepchildren are not enough. And I just think if people really loved children and just wanted a family unit, then there are orphanages around the world packed with children who need homes. But it's not about that. Kids are an extension of themselves, so that plays in my head when people throw out the 'selfish' thing."

Theresa's response typified that of my other respondents: "Selfishness is by far the most unfair and tiresome assumption people make. They assume we are rolling in cash and live in a mansion and take lavish holidays every year. Ha! I wish." Theresa called it the "default assumption," and although this annoyed her to no end, she realized people had no basis to believe otherwise: "They don't know me. They don't know the dollars I give to charity. They don't know the time I devote to women's issues. They don't know that I will drop everything to come to the aid of my friends and family."

As my survey revealed, there are many reasons why someone might choose childlessness. Yet selfishness remains the assumed motive, despite a lack of evidence to support that claim.

A 1998 British study of childless men and women, conducted by Fiona McAllister and Lynda Clarke at the Family Policy Studies Center, concluded that "childfree people were not self-centered individuals. The absence of children did not necessarily mean the absence of other caring responsibilities." This was true in my own sample of interview subjects as well. I encountered many voluntarily childless people who, like Nick and Diane (profiled in Chapter 5), had taken responsibility for the care of elderly parents and other relatives, or had harbored young relatives for long periods, or had adopted at-risk animals or mentored at-risk children.

McAllister and Clarke's study also found that "a rejection of parenthood was not matched by a rejection of children's place in society. Most childless people were in favour of supporting children through taxes."[2] So why, in the face of studies proving otherwise, do these stereotypes persist?

Blame it on our culture. Despite the fact that we see little evidence of child-centric government policies or funding, our culture remains pronatalist, and our perception of intentional childlessness is filtered through that lens.

In her paper titled "Choosing Childlessness," sociologist Kristin Park wrote, "The general influence of pronatalist beliefs can be seen in the negative evaluations of the intentionally childless that are documented in many studies. Compared to the involuntarily childless and to parents, the voluntarily childless are seen as less socially desirable, less well-adjusted, less nurturant, and less mature, as well as more materialistic, more selfish, and more individualistic."[3]

Perception is everything, and the childfree will continue to be characterized this way until we confront these notions. Below are some of the most common assumptions about the childfree (outside of selfishness) that can—and should—be challenged.

ASSUMPTION 1:
THE CHILDLESS BY CHOICE DON'T LIKE KIDS

Let me start by saying that yes, there is a minority of the childless by choice who do admit to having an aversion to children. And some would even go so far as to confess that they'd be happy if a child never entered their orbit. Some have chosen not to have kids because they can't tolerate the noise and the chaos small children typically bring to an environment, or because, frankly, they simply don't like them. And aren't we glad they made that decision?

Personally, I happen to think that not wanting to be around kids is an excellent reason for not having them. We all know people who can't stand kids but had them anyway—perhaps not intentionally, but the result is the same. I had a boyfriend in high school whose mother passed away when he was a child, leaving him alone with a remote and neglectful father who really didn't like children—any children, not even his only son. While we were dating, I rarely saw his father outside of his favorite chair and never heard him speak more than two sentences to his son or to me.

I suspected this man had more serious and pressing problems than simply disliking children, but I did feel sorry for his son. So I applaud those people who have the level of self-awareness and honesty to admit that they just plain don't like kids and take the necessary steps to ensure they don't have them. As the Aussies say, "Good on ya, mate!"

If parents need proof that the childfree hate kids, they don't have to look far. Many of the childfree websites offer forums or safe places in which the childfree can rant about injustices in the tax code, "family-friendly" workplace benefits that exclude childfree families, and unruly children and their "breeder" parents. Some of the vitriolic comments I see on these sites make me squirm, but I have learned these opinions are just that: one person's opinion. Personally, I don't like the word "breed" or "breeder." I don't use it in reference to humans, because it reduces to a mindless biological imperative something that many parents feel is a very profound event.

If you looked solely to the Internet to gauge how the childfree regard children, you might very well come away with the impression that we all hate kids. Yet a dislike of children is not typical of the majority of the childless by choice I have interviewed and surveyed. Actually, I was surprised by how many of the voluntarily childless I met during the course of my research who had actively sought jobs or volunteer work that involved them in regular interactions with children. I met daycare workers, teachers, child advocates, social workers, tutors, mentors, and, yes, even a professional clown.

"Being childless by choice doesn't mean you hate kids," wrote Jodi. "In fact, my friends' children are smart, funny, loving, interesting people who just happen to be kids."

What I have come to understand after many years of studying the childless by choice is that the decision to remain childless is typically not a rejection of children so much as it is a rejection of cultural norms, assumptions, and ideals that support parenthood as the normative life course over all other options.

So please, don't assume all childfree people hate kids. Invite them to your child's birthday party or ask them if they would like to coach or mentor or—yikes!—even baby-sit once in a while. They may politely decline your invitation, or they may surprise you and become the best coach or baby sitter you could ever hope for.

ASSUMPTION 2:
THE CHILDLESS BY CHOICE ARE IMMATURE

One of the reasons why many of us actually enjoy children's company is that we are reluctant to let go of the pursuits of our youth that continue to give us pleasure. Perhaps this is why the childfree are often labeled immature, but I like to call it being young at heart.

Anthony, an army officer and pilot, met his wife, Sara, through their college skydiving club, and they have been jumping into, and out of, planes ever since. Trond and Roz still love getting down and dirty and being silly, and look forward to weekends with their friends who have kids, saying, "We teach them how to play." Even though I was a reluctant baby sitter, kids always loved it when I came to baby-sit because I never tired of playing dress-up.

Okay, so maybe we *are* immature, but not in the way we are often perceived as and criticized for being—as slackers who are afraid to grow up and take on adult responsibilities. The assumption that the only path to responsible adulthood is parenthood is another tired remnant of a pronatalist culture that clearly does not hold a stitch. For the past five minutes, I have been sitting in front of my computer, mining my gray matter for a memory of one childfree person who might be described as a slacker. As I flip through my mental Rolodex, I recall CEOs, financial analysts, military careerists, nurses, professors, teachers, farmers, filmmakers, pharmacists, IT professionals, and engineers, but no one who was still living in their parents' home, unwilling to step up and be a self-sustaining and productive adult in the world.

ASSUMPTION 3:
THE CHILDLESS BY CHOICE ARE UNFULFILLED

There is this image, perpetuated in films and in literature, of the tragically lonely and unfulfilled person being redeemed, or given new life, by the introduction of a child into their world. The crone of our fairy tales is always a childless woman, portrayed as cranky, isolated, and feared. The childless man on the big screen is successful on the surface but unhappy, self-centered, and blissfully unaware of how bereft of soulful purpose his life is until he becomes a father or takes on the father role for a needy child. The primary staple of celebrity magazines is the story of the sex- or substance-addicted rock star who finally agrees to check into rehab because of the transformative effects of fathering a child. If I didn't know better, I would think that the twelve-step program now has a thirteenth step: Have a kid.

It plays well. The cute kid as a transformative tool is a lot more fun than a cancer diagnosis, though both are useful if you want to motivate a character to reassess his priorities. So maybe that's why the path to fulfillment is clogged with strollers—because our cultural stories make it so. In contrast, most of the stories about childless people are predictably tragic: They die alone, unloved or unlovable, or they commit suicide.

This characterization of the childless contrasts starkly with what I heard and saw as I traveled through North America. One thing that struck me as I reviewed the transcripts and video of my interviews was how generally content people professed to be. There was very little evidence of dissatisfaction, or hoping and wanting. Mark, age forty-six, expressed it this way: "I'm married. I don't have kids. I don't see a void, I just see my life." Sara, age twenty-nine, said, "I feel very fulfilled as a person, and as part of a couple, just the way we are."

Theresa felt she needed to debunk this common myth. "Our lives are not empty because we lack children. On the contrary, we have more time and energy for other things to enhance our lives."

ASSUMPTION 4:
THE CHILDLESS BY CHOICE WILL REGRET
THEIR DECISION NOT TO HAVE CHILDREN

Every time I had the chance to interview a childless by choice couple, I asked the question "Have you ever regretted your decision not to have kids?" No one admitted feeling regretful, though Debb did confess one small thing: She thought her husband would have been a great adult for a little kid to grow up around. He disagreed.

Every other voluntarily childless person I spoke with either said, "No, I've never regretted not having kids" or acknowledged fleeting twinges, or the possibility, of regret. "Call me in thirty/forty/fifty/sixty years and I'll tell you," they would say. The people I interviewed were all under the age of seventy, and the prospect of remorse seemed far off for them.

The concerns most people had about their childlessness were not the threat of regret, but rather things like "What do I do when I am alone and I can't take care of myself?" or "Who's going to get all my stuff?" Loneliness was not a major concern. Many of the people I spoke with had an extensive social or family network in place to assist them when they needed help or companionship. Some were already funding long-term care and imagined they would end up being cared for by private nurses or in a residential facility of some sort at the end of their life.

These people thought it was crazy—not to mention just plain wrong—for people to have kids just so they would have someone to take care of them when they got old. As Kathy pointed out, elder care in the United States is provided increasingly by people who aren't blood relatives. I did a bit of investigating and, sure enough, I found that adult children represent only 37 percent of elder-care providers in the United States.[4]

Jennifer was in a childfree marriage for five years before she lost her husband to a heart attack. "When Dan died, people would say, 'I bet you regret not having kids, now that he's gone'—not even phrasing it like a question. Sometimes I would respond and say, 'No, actually, I am so grateful that I do not find myself a single mom now.' Dan's death really did help validate my decision. I had to spend a lot of time during the grief process learning about myself and what I want the rest of my life to look like—and kids were nowhere in there." Biological kids, that is, since Jennifer ultimately ended up embracing a stepmom role when she later married a man with grown children.

Jennifer was in her mid-thirties when we corresponded. Does regret come only with advanced age? I wondered. Again, I turned to the studies.

A Canadian study conducted by Sherryl Jeffries and Candace Konnert compared the regret and psychological well-being of seventy-two women over the age of forty-five who were voluntarily childless, involuntarily childless, or mothers. When it came to evaluating psychological well-being, Jeffries and Konnert found that "the voluntarily childless women had the highest total scores (indicating greater well-being), mothers scored slightly lower, and the involuntarily childless women had the lowest scores." When it came to regret, they reported, "Among the voluntarily childless women, all but one reported either no current child-related regrets, or regret that was 'minor,' 'fleeting,' or 'more of a curiosity than a regret.' Almost all reported no change or less regret with age, or that they were even more convinced that their decision to remain childless was the right decision."[5]

This was also true for Sue, an early articulator, who told me that the thing that most validated her choice to have a tubal ligation at age twenty-six was the fact that "I am completely at peace with my decision thirty-one years later. I can honestly say at age fifty-seven that not having children was one of the best decisions I've ever made in my life. I have absolutely no regrets, and don't anticipate any."

Sylvia was also fifty-seven when I interviewed her, and was concerned about aging issues, as she was currently without a partner and was an only child. "The only regret I have is that there will be no one to look out for me in my old age, or pass my belongings down to. I have the fear of lying in my home, dead for days, before someone realizes it." But then she countered, "When I hear about all the problems people have with their children, I do not miss having children in the least."

The specter of regret seems to be a cultural assumption more than a real fear harbored by the childfree. I heard many stories of couples being warned by their families and peers that they'd rue their decision, but observed very little evidence of this sentiment among the childless by choice themselves.

ASSUMPTION 5:
THE DECISION NOT TO HAVE KIDS IS AN EASY ONE

The suggestion that not a lot of thought goes into the decision to remain childless ranks right up there with selfishness as a common but unfounded assessment of childfree motives and processes.

"The myth that we made the decision lightly really annoys the hell out of me," said Debb. "We spent hours and hours talking about whether we wanted kids—the costs and the benefits. We researched the issue. I wrote an honors thesis on the topic." Her husband, Mark, agreed: "When people make the decision not to have children, it is very thought out, probably more so than the decision *to* have kids."

Misty described her process: "I have thought more about having children than anyone else I know. I knew I never had the desire in the first place, and I had to examine what I would gain, or miss out on, based on my decision." However, the word "decision" didn't feel right to Misty, either. "I don't know if it was so much a decision as a realization of something that was already there." Either way, it was something she had thought long and hard about because she had realized, as she put it, "how little I had in common with people who wanted kids."

Tamara understood that every choice a person makes has consequences, and that making a choice moves other options off the table. This is true if you choose to have kids or if you choose not to. "One problem with mainstream American culture is that we take these words 'freedom' and 'choice' to mean we should have choices about everything all of the time, but that's not the case. When you choose something, it locks you into a path. The freedom was once there, but when you've chosen, you have to accept the consequences. It's not like, 'Wait a minute, I don't like these consequences; where's my choice?' You've already made it."

ASSUMPTION 6:
THE CHILDLESS BY CHOICE ARE MATERIALISTIC

I blame this assumption on the unknown person who coined the acronym DINK—double income, no kids. This term is used to describe a relatively affluent, childless demographic, but more often is used, like "yuppie," to describe a lifestyle associated with conspicuous consumption and materialism.

This is how the DINK demographic was characterized in an article featured on Time.com:

"The members of this newly defined species can best be spotted after 9 PM in gourmet groceries, their Burberry-clothed arms reaching for the arugula or a Le Menu frozen flounder dinner. In the parking lot, they slide into their BMWs and lift cellular phones to their ears before zooming off to their architect-designed houses in the exurbs. After warmly greeting Rover (often an akita or golden retriever), they check to be sure the pooch service has delivered his nutritionally correct dog food. Then they consult the phone-answering machine, pop dinner into the microwave, and finally sink into their Italian leather sofa to watch a videocassette of, say, last week's *L.A. Law* or *Cheers* on their high-definition, large-screen stereo television."[6]

A tad over the top, don't you think? However, this is the vision people conjure up when the term "DINK" is invoked. Last I checked, double incomes were the norm for most families of two, or four, in North America. Gone are the days when one person's income can support the average household living above the poverty line. We can no longer assume (if we ever could) that the two-income childless or childfree household has the discretionary dollars, or the inclination, to fund the kind of lifestyle described above.

The reason why you might find more DINKs in the gourmet-grocery store after 9:00 PM is that they likely work full-time and can't shop during business hours. They might work longer hours than their coworkers who have children, sometimes because parents have to go to a recital or catch a soccer game. To the consternation of millions of single, childless, and childfree persons, the people who are expected to stay behind are them.

I've lost count of the complaints I've heard from the childfree that their coworkers take advantage of their parent status to get off early or work fewer hours. This type of discrimination is well documented on childfree websites and in books like Elinor Burkett's *The Baby Boon: How Family-Friendly America Cheats the Childless.* Claudia, an executive with a Fortune 500 company, wrote to me and said it was unfair to assume "that since we don't have children we can work 24/7! Life is more than work . . . even for the childless." Yet parents don't appear to sympathize. They are struggling and in a time crunch, and many imagine you have no life outside of work. You don't have kids?! *What do you do?*

The childfree, on average, do have more free time and discretionary income than their parenting counterparts, but what they do with that time and money is likely quite different from what the *Time* magazine article described. In my survey and interviews, I did not ask what income bracket my respondents fell into. However, I did interview most couples in their homes, so I can say, truthfully, that I saw zero architect-designed mansions or purebred dogs with concierge services. What I saw most often were modest homes or apartments, and pets rescued from shelters.

Most of the people described as DINKs will become parents one day, and will willingly give up a good chunk of their discretionary income to their children. They won't stop buying, they'll just buy differently: They'll get tickets to Disneyland instead of Dubrovnik; they'll choose the SUV over the sporty hybrid; they'll invest in college funds rather than Roth IRAs. Some go into serious debt to fund their expanding family, which is one reason why married couples with children are more than twice as likely to go bankrupt than are childfree couples (according to a survey of 2,200 U.S. families conducted by Elizabeth Warren and Amelia Warren Tyagi).[7]

So what do the childfree spend their extra dollars on— that is, those who actually have something left after paying the bills? Based entirely on my observation, it's travel, hobbies, housing, relatives, pets, and charitable donations.

Angie and her husband, Mike, saw their disposable income not as another reason to remain childless, but as a side benefit, and they were strategic about how they spent their money. Mike thought he would make a good father, but, like Angie, he was ambivalent about parenthood. When they ultimately encountered fertility issues, they decided to accept their fate. "While we had options and so much new medical technology available to us, we did not opt to use it," said Angie. "We'd known other couples who were in panic mode, trying every possible, expensive method to conceive, without success. We also opted out of adoption. I guess we sort of felt that this was 'meant to be' for us and got on with other aspects of our lives."

Angie and Mike had given many hours and dollars to their favorite causes. "My husband and I agree that you do not have to be a parent to be a positive influence on a child's life. Volunteering with organizations like Big Brothers Big Sisters, family shelters, and charitable organizations are some examples of how we contribute. Also, our position as a childless couple allows us to donate more to charitable organizations— likely much more than the average family would even consider contributing."

ASSUMPTION 7:
PETS ARE CHILD SUBSTITUTES FOR THE CHILDFREE

The one part of this stereotype I cannot challenge is the fact that the majority of the childless by choice I encountered had at least one pet.

But really, are these animals standing in for children? I don't think so. People see actress Betty White with her "babies" on those 1-800-PetMeds advertisements and presume these pampered animals are child substitutes for the childless. They are not. Jerry made the distinction, suggesting pets may be *better* than kids. "Having a pet is almost like having children," he said. "But unlike human children, your pet will likely never experiment with dangerous drugs, and as long as a pet is spayed or neutered, you need never fear that it will come home pregnant or make other animals pregnant."

Rob did acknowledge that "our pets are our kids," but he rejected the notion that they are child "substitutes."

"I wouldn't use that word," he told me. "When I say that our pets are our kids, I'm saying they are important and loved and part of the family. It's frustrating when a pet dies and someone says, 'It's only a pet' or, 'You can get another one next week.' Try saying that to a parent."

Although the childless by choice couples I interviewed clearly cherished their pets, I did not see any diamond-studded collars or shrines to Fluffy. I did see a lot of found or rescued animals of questionable pedigree. Wayne and Gina had even adopted a family of feral cats that they went to feed daily in an abandoned lot next to their local Wal-Mart. They were afraid that if they didn't feed them, Wal-Mart management would call Animal Control and they'd be euthanized.

Many people did point to their pets and say, "This is my nurturing outlet." They enjoyed the give-and-take of the pet-human relationship, and some even referred to each other as Daddy or Mommy to their pets. This sometimes perplexed the people's parents, who had observed how well their sons and daughters cared for their pets and, unsatisfied with the furry grandchild, requested the "real" grandchild. But these pet owners were all acutely aware that caring for a pet and raising a child were completely different tours of duty.

ASSUMPTION 8:
EVERYONE IS CAPABLE OF BEING A "GOOD" PARENT

While I was writing this chapter, the Nebraska state legislature was about to amend its new "safe haven" law, which allowed parents to abandon their children at hospitals without suffering legal consequences for abandonment. In the five months after the original law took effect, thirty-five kids were left at Nebraska hospitals, most of them adolescents. The state legislature held a special session to change the language of the law to limit the age of the abandoned child to thirty days in order to reflect the law's original intent.[8]

Despite the weekly news reports and media portraits of overwhelmed or abusive parents, horrific custody battles, desperate housewives, and deadbeat dads, there is a lingering assumption that all people are capable of parenting and should be encouraged to do so.

Yet many of the people I interviewed didn't feel they would make good parents for any number of reasons, or they felt they were unable, or unwilling, to make the sacrifices or the changes to their lifestyle that would be necessary to be responsible parents. Others felt strongly that the desire for a child is a prerequisite for parenthood; without desire, many of the people I surveyed felt there was no choice, believing that it is morally wrong to risk getting pregnant if you are not going to happily welcome a child into your life.

Kristin summed it up perfectly. "It bothers me when people assume the worst motives for the decision. Like childfree people just can't be bothered with the sacrifices or hassles of parenting, or that we want to do lots of material consumption instead, or take long vacations. Few people seem to be able to give credit that the decision might have been thoughtfully made based on an honest appraisal of one's priorities, personality type, skills, or goals. If parenthood is a role that everyone is supposed to adopt, that doesn't allow for people to be inclined toward it—or not—at the outset. Rather, it's claimed that you learn the skills and adopt, or are transformed toward, the necessary temperament on the job."

The childless by choice I interviewed believed it was risky to assume effective parenting is something you learn on the job. What happens if you are wrong and turn out not to be a good parent? And really, isn't it a bit naive to assume that the well-being of your child is entirely under your control?

Angie had an older sister whose marriage ended in divorce, leaving her with three children. "I think the risk factor of knowing that so many marriages end in divorce, and the odds that women are most often the parent who ends up raising children alone, had a big influence on me. Another factor in this decision-making process was working with troubled children and teens after college." Angie had spent much of her career in public health. "To me, it was frightening and sad to see what the kids, as well as the parents, were going through. Despite the fact that some parents worked so hard to do everything right, in the end it was peer pressure and society that became the major influence. It was quite eye-opening. While I'm not sure that this experience was a primary factor in remaining childless, it certainly had some impact on my view of parenthood."

The childless by choice could not ignore that fact that even those parents who want children and try to be good parents sometimes fail to raise healthy and happy children or are severely overwhelmed by the task. Neither was a desirable outcome, and many of my participants recognized that their lack of enthusiasm for parenthood, coupled with a perceived lack of skills or aptitude, increased their risk of failure.

CHALLENGING THE DEFAULT

In the absence of information on the real motives for voluntary childlessness, the "default" assumptions hold sway. If you've never had a serious conversation with a childfree person about their reasons for or the consequences of childlessness, how would you know what was fact and what was fiction? And what would you think if the answer were simply "I never wanted to be a parent"?

If the fear-based myths and preconceived notions about a childfree life—regret, arrested development, lack of fulfillment—don't apply to the majority of the voluntarily childless, what does?

After years of research and interviews, I am tempted to say contentment does, but that state of being is sometimes marred by others' perception that it can't be authentic. How can you be a happy, fully realized adult without kids?

In a pronatalist society, anyone who rejects the default of parenthood or admits to being less than thrilled about the prospect of being a parent is often perceived as a "child hater" or "selfish." These assumptions, and our minority status, put the childfree squarely in the category of "outsider" and are likely why the childless by choice still experience stigmatization in North America.

Compared with other, more visible minorities, the childfree do not experience as much overt discrimination or exclusion on a daily basis. Like our gay and lesbian peers, we have found that we can assimilate fairly well, provided we hide our status from those who might take issue with what some people call a deviant lifestyle. This is not the ideal solution, of course. The childfree, like all minority groups, hope for a time when we can be accepted for who we are and how we live, but that time will come only as a result of empathy and some level of understanding. In the meantime, we find ways to adapt as we live on the margins. We find like-minded peers and communities who embrace or validate us. However, there remains the challenge of finding acceptance for the childfree life in the culture of the majority, in a society that idealizes parenthood for all its citizens. And as long as the rationales for choosing this life appear defective or are misunderstood or simply imagined, the entire decision-making process (along with those who make the unsanctioned choice) is going to be perceived as flawed by some.

This is why I feel it is important to challenge the myths and tell the truth about life without kids. In the following chapters, we'll explore the culture in which we live, how the childless and childfree adapt—or not—within its confines, and the disadvantages of a childfree life.

CHAPTER 7

Childless in Babyville:
Navigating a Pronatalist World

It's 2004. Actress Gwyneth Paltrow is beaming from her perch on the familiar yellow sofa on the set of *The Oprah Winfrey Show*. Are they talking about her latest movie? Her favorite costars? No, Oprah wants to talk about Gwyneth's experience as a new mom. She's just given birth to her first child—a baby girl—and everyone is dying to know why she and her husband, rock star Chris Martin, named the kid Apple.

If you have any doubt that we live in a pronatalist world, you need only flip though celebrity and fashion magazines to see how art directors use naked infants to "sex up" their layouts and ads. We are in the midst of an A-list baby boom in which the cherub-cheeked baby has replaced the designer-clad pocket dog as Hollywood's accessory of choice.

Fast-forward to 2008. Gwyneth Paltrow has had a second child and laments, "My son did say the word 'paparazzi' the other day, and he's only two." We're still in the throes of a baby love-fest: Magazines feature "bump alerts," and photographers can expect to fetch significantly more cash for their celebrity photos if they get the kid in the frame. In April 2008, Forbes.com featured an article on the most expensive baby pictures, fueled by the rumor that *People* magazine paid $6 million for exclusive first photos of Jennifer Lopez and Marc Anthony's twins.

Although notable in its excess, this manifestation of pronatalism is not new. For the childless and childfree, however, it's unsettling to see the mainstream media ignoring their growing demographic. Leslie Lafayette, in her book *Why Don't You Have Kids?*, had this to say in her chapter entitled "Living Childfree Isn't for Sissies!":

> *"By 2010, projects American Demographics magazine, the number of married couples without children is expected to increase by nearly 50 percent to nearly 31 million. It's clear there's a trend here.*
>
> *Now, cup your hand to your ear. Listen carefully. What do you hear? Babies. Goo-goo and Ga-ga. Poo-poo and ka-ka. Magazine articles and TV ads, disposable diapers and breast-feeding techniques, sitcoms and movies, voices from the pulpit, voices from the legislature, family values and family size and family discounts . . . all celebrating the wonders of procreation.*
>
> *All well and good . . . but what's a nonparenting adult to do?"[1]*

Indeed, choosing a life without kids isn't for sissies. Expect a certain amount of frustration, alienation, marginalization, and misunderstanding when you encounter people who don't understand why you would choose to be childless.

Expect that you will be stigmatized for making the choice to remain childfree.

FAMILY, GOD, AND COUNTRY

The reality that millions of happily married couples are choosing not to have kids is hard for many to understand. Long-standing societal conventions are challenged when couples choose childlessness. In addition, childlessness has long been associated with regret and grief, loneliness and immaturity. Parenthood is seen as the norm, the path to responsible, mature adulthood and citizenship.

Pronatalism buttresses these stereotypes. The ideology aspect of pronatalism can be a powerful force, particularly for those on the fence, or those governed by pronatalist laws, or those whose primary community is in the church or temple.

In North America and globally, religion and culture have strongly influenced pronatalism. In the Catholic faith, refusal to have children is grounds for an annulment. (Ironically, the most culturally acceptable form of remaining childless is to become a priest or a nun.) Jewish law says a man should seek a divorce if the marriage has been childless after ten years.

Religious pronatalism is often couched in terms of the political and the patriotic, particularly during times of economic uncertainty or war.

In the 1930s, when contraceptive use was on the rise among married couples in England and France, and when the eugenics movement had strong support in academic circles and in Nazi Germany, H. L. Goudge, professor of divinity at the University of Oxford, had this to say to an audience of Anglican clergypeople who had gathered in Manchester, England:

> *"The great outstanding evil is the widespread refusal of parenthood among all classes except the one where it is least to be desired. England, like France, is choosing the path of national suicide. Now as to this, not only all Christians, but all lovers of their country, are at one.*
>
> *We have to preach not only the beauty and glory of fatherhood and motherhood, but the duty of it. If there is anything more to be detested than contraceptives, it is the selfishness and cowardice which generally lead to their use."*[2]

In the context of current debates over same-sex marriages, immigration, and party politics, new spins on pronatalist arguments are being put forth, but the underlying fears appear not to have changed.

Many have argued that same-sex couples should not be allowed to marry because they cannot procreate, though many do, using donor eggs or sperm, or surrogates. Since many heterosexual couples use these same methods to conceive and bear their children, social conservatives who put forth these arguments risk alienating the very people they claim to serve.

In 2005, Republicans were gleefully predicting that Democrats would soon be extinct, citing a Pew Research Center report that found that twice as many staunch conservatives were married with children in the household than were liberals.[3] The following year, *The Wall Street Journal* published an article with the subtitle "Liberal politics will prove fruitless as long as liberals refuse to multiply."[4] It's unclear whether these opinions actually influence fertility; however, they do illustrate how pronatalist ideology is tinged by politics, bigotry, or fear, as evidenced by the message, articulated or implied, that "we want more of us and less of you."

Although North Americans have the liberty—defended by laws—to remain childless or childfree, they may not have the approval of their community to do so. When I interviewed Duke University demographer and sociologist Dr. S. Philip Morgan, he explained why: "Sociologists talk about norms. You know there's a norm when there is a sanction or a punishment that goes along with it. So if there's a norm that people should have children, should be parents, if people don't do it, then they should be sanctioned or punished in some way. Much of our behavior is guided by informal approval or disapproval of people around us. It's non-normative to say, 'I don't have children, and I don't want any,' and if you say that in several different environments, you will feel the sanctions."[5]

Those of us who are childless by choice know we are "non-normative." While our cultural icons are touting the joys of parenthood, we are doubling up on contraceptives or getting snipped. Our culture is selling parenthood, but we're not buying.

SLAYING THE BEASTS

What's clear from all the studies, including mine, is that the cultural myths that support parenthood as the most viable and normative life course toward the development of a mature, responsible, and fulfilled adult are being challenged by the childless by choice.

In Chapter 3, I identified three expectations or beliefs that are submerged in our cultural permafrost. These are the ancient beasts that the childless by choice, in the course of their decision making and soul searching, have exposed to closer scrutiny and pronounced extinct. To recap:

- Mammoth number one is the expectation that we will all become parents one day and it will be a rewarding experience.
- Mammoth number two is the idea that parenthood is a critical stage in human development and maturity.
- Mammoth number three is the belief that all couples should be encouraged to parent, regardless of their ability or desire.

Let's examine these ideas one at a time. First, imagine if every person on the planet wanted and expected to be a parent one day (to a certain extent, this isn't a what-if scenario—the assumption that everyone wants to have children certainly exists). Aside from the massive toll that would take on our planet, given the inordinate number of people already inhabiting it, what happens for those who don't have children? Are they inclined or prompted to experience feelings of disappointment or regret simply because the population expects this of them?

Untold numbers of women and men who always imagined they would be parents are now childless by circumstance. Are they destined for a life of disappointment? And what happens to the rest of us, the couples who never seriously considered parenthood for themselves, or couples who postponed kids and then decided life is good just the way it is—the childless by choice?

According to a 2002 United Nations Population Division report, the United States has the highest proportion of childless women by age forty: 20 percent.[6] And yes, childlessness is on the rise all over the world due to a number of factors, including infertility and delayed marriage and childbearing. So this mammoth assumption that everyone will have children eventually, and that doing so is the most positive outcome, is bad not only for the planet, but also for those of us who are comfortable with our choice not to be parents and those who find themselves childless by circumstance. The childless by choice reject the assumption of parenthood because it excludes so many of us and implies a less-than status or a less-than experience for those who are not parents. It also dismisses our current reality: We can no longer assume parenthood is a given.

The childless by choice—as well as people who are parents—are also questioning the notion that parenthood will be rewarding for all, based on their experiences, observations, and interactions with family and peers. As a culture, we expect rewards from parenting that often aren't realized, causing some parents to feel regret or shame, or complain—or, in Joe Sindoni's case, write a book that honestly assesses the pros and cons of parenthood. Sindoni, who received full custody of his two infant sons and raised them to adulthood, wrote *50*

Reasons Not to Have Kids: And What to Do If You Have Them Anyway in part because he wanted people to realize, going in, that "there certainly is a lot of good and a lot of responsibility in raising children, but the trials and tribulations often outweigh the good."[7]

Nick, the early articulator profiled in Chapter 5, recalls that in the first ten years of his marriage to Diane, "our childbearing friends were always peer-pressuring us to have children. Then, when I saw one of them in a particularly stressful moment rearing their kids, I would always say, 'See there, now you know why I don't have kids.' And they would invariably catch themselves and say something like 'Oh, it's so rewarding.' And for them, maybe it is, and good for them, but we can't see the reward, personally."

In 2008, Rabbi Shmuley, hosting his show on the Oprah & Friends satellite radio channel, asked his listeners to consider this question: If they had to do it all over again knowing what they know now, would they have kids again? This was a man who had eight kids and a ninth on the way, and had made a career of counseling troubled families. The rabbi acknowledged that in his and others' experience as a parent, "the return on the investment—it just isn't there." Why? Because we have expectations—expectations of the joys of parenthood, which do exist, but perhaps not in such a quantity or quality as to balance out the stress, sacrifice, and hardships that come along with the parenting role.

When self-help guru Dr. Phil McGraw surveyed more than twenty thousand parents for his book *Family First,* nearly one-third agreed with the statement "If I knew then what I know now, I probably wouldn't have had children."[8] "Shocking," responded former U.S. president George W. Bush when Dr. Phil shared this fact with him[9]—but not so shocking to the childless by choice, who have conducted their own informal surveys while deciding whether to have kids.

When Lou's girlfriend, Jessica, informed him that she didn't want to have children, Lou left her for a month, went on a "soul search," and began asking his friends in the military about their experience as parents. What he heard—stories about stress and marital conflicts—convinced Lou that he didn't want kids either, a conviction that had not changed in his twenty-three years of marriage to Jessica.

Lou and Jessica are a couple who also challenge the second mammoth: that parenthood is a critical stage in human development and maturity. As the primary caregiver for Jessica, who suffers from chronic pain, Lou knows what it is like to have a dependent. As a career military man who has been stationed around the world, he has had his share of responsibilities for those under his command and care. As a marathon runner, he understands the need to sacrifice time, energy, and sweat to achieve a goal. Hardly someone who might be described as immature or irresponsible.

Elaine felt it was time to challenge another myth that is an offshoot of mammoth number two: "that we are somehow defective or deviant because we don't want kids. The latter is mostly pervasive within the counseling and psychology community."

The mental-health community and social scientists often regard parenthood as a life stage, or a stepping-stone on the path to fully realized adulthood. If you believe this, you might wonder how people who remain childless earn their stripes in the world. However, if parenthood is in fact a critical stage in human development and maturity, how do we explain away people like Lou, who happily embrace formidable challenges and responsibilities yet choose to remain childless? What do we do with people like TV executive and host Oprah Winfrey, author Jane Austen, philanthropist and chocolate-company founder Milton Hershey, activist Rosa Parks, astronaut and educator Sally Ride, and actress Helen Mirren? Or people like jazz legend Louis Armstrong, who adopted his cousin's mentally disabled child when the boy was orphaned at three years old? Can we marginalize their experiences or their contributions because they—whether by choice or by circumstance—did not raise biological offspring?

How do they evaluate their own lives? Before Armstrong's death, he told his biographer, "I think I had a beautiful life. I didn't wish for anything I couldn't get, and I got pretty near everything I wanted because I worked for it."[10]

When award-winning actress Dame Helen Mirren was interviewed on *60 Minutes,* correspondent Morley Safer asked, "Do you regret that you've never had children?" Mirren responded, "No, absolutely not. Absolutely not. I am so happy that I didn't have children . . . because I've had freedom."[11] Freedom to bounce between homes in England, France, and the United States; freedom to enjoy and nourish her two loves—her work in film and theater and her extended family, comprising a husband, stepsons, a sister, nephews, and longtime friends. In her book *In the Frame,* she writes, "I am often asked where I consider to be home, and I really have no answer for that. . . . My home is wherever this motley clan . . . collect, and become as one."[12]

Anthony, an active-duty U.S. Army officer, remembered a rare, quiet moment during a mission when two young soldiers who had served with him for a few years inquired about his childless status. He recalled one soldier's saying, "'Sir, I just found out you don't have children.' And I said, 'Well, no, guys, I have you.' And these two just looked at each other, like, *Oh, okay, that makes sense.* I didn't think about it much at the time. I was really just giving them a hard time. But when they understood that, I felt it kind of validated my decision, that perhaps the way I conduct myself while on duty and in service to our country does cover every bit of the gap, if you want to call it a gap, in not having children."

Moving on to the third and final mammoth—the one that, by my reckoning, the intentionally childless slay universally— is the idea that all couples should be encouraged to parent, regardless of ability or desire. Here is where Lou, the man who imagined he would end up a dad until he met Jessica, strongly begs to differ. He doesn't know why, but he knows for certain that he doesn't have the parenting instinct. He is convinced that if he were a father, he wouldn't be able to give his children what they needed.

Trond disagreed that parenting should be endorsed for all couples; rather, he urged people to think it through. "I've heard too many people say they got married and had kids because they didn't know there was another way to be. I'm not saying that what I'm doing is right for everyone, but for those people who have a nagging doubt that the parenting thing is not for them, they should be encouraged to look at the alternatives. Not everyone should be a parent."

Rachel believed she could better serve the world by not having kids. "At age twenty-seven, I was diagnosed with cancer and needed surgery. My choice was simple: I could put it off and fairly safely have a child or two with my husband over the next couple of years, or I could have the surgery immediately and eliminate my ability to have children forever. I opted for the latter." Why? Rachel felt strongly that the world was already overpopulated; she had also observed her friends with children and knew that lifestyle wasn't for her. "I've seen how children consume their parents' lives, and my husband and I don't want any part of it."

Dan felt the same way. "The lifestyle of my parents was so uninspiring that I wanted none of it." So he dropped out, rejecting the lifestyle he was brought up in, and took on a number of jobs—including commercial diving and fishing and rigging tall ships—that kept him away from home and exposed him to the kind of physical risks that have left many a child fatherless. "I was interested in enjoying freedom and pursuing a life of dangerous, exciting work and play that is not appropriate to parenting." Dan agreed to be interviewed because he understood people often do what is expected of them. "I want to help those caught between expectations and personal goals and desires to find solace and strength," he told me.

Why do we, the childfree, need solace and strength? Because we are standing up to assumptions, beliefs, and ideals long held by the majority, which includes our family, friends, and neighbors. The choice we make to remain childless flies in the face of everything mainstream culture claims to value. We are rocking the boat, and I suspect this is why the backlash against the childless by choice sometimes seems disproportionate to our actual impact.

Dr. S. Philip Morgan helped me understand the "visceral reaction" to intentional childlessness. By questioning "the notion that parenthood is a good thing," the childless by choice create what he called a "clash of values." Worst-case motives are ascribed to the childfree because "people don't know the details, and at some level they don't want to know the details," of why people might choose childlessness, because "it's a fundamental challenge to the way most people see the world."[13]

When is a personal, private decision an affront to others? When it challenges everything they know or believe, or when the decision, or your defense of it, incurs judgment or alarming and dire warnings: "You'll get breast cancer, you'll die neglected and alone, you'll change your mind, you'll regret it."

Yet couples are increasingly choosing childlessness, swimming against the current, battling doubt and stigmas to make a choice that feels right to them. Why? Because they believe that parenthood is not for everyone, and, more important, that it's not for them.

OUR CULTURE'S RESPONSE TO
INTENTIONAL CHILDLESSNESS

So what happens when you start telling people that you're childless by choice?

The intentionally childless experience a plethora of reactions, including curiosity, suspicion, wrongful assumptions, defensiveness, avoidance, discomfort, rejection, marginalization, discrimination, prejudice, pity, envy, and support.

For me, curiosity is the response I welcome most, as it allows me to articulate my real motives, confirm that my childless status is intentional, and avoid people's assumption that I'm tragically infertile and their accompanying look of pity: "Oh, don't worry, you're still young" or, even worse, "I'll pray for you," intimating that my status is so dire as to require divine intervention.

Suspicion usually results from unfair presumptions, and typically those who harbor them won't announce them in your presence. In my opinion, this reticence is unfortunate, since it robs you of the opportunity to challenge these presumptions. Jennifer understood that most people she encountered would never know the truth about why she'd decided to remain childfree. "It is mostly casual acquaintances who are the ones who question it, so I generally don't get to talk to them about what their underlying assumptions are. I'm guessing from reactions that they consider me selfish, or just out of touch with my deeply hidden maternal instinct, and that I will change my mind eventually."

Assumptions may also lead to avoidance, in the form of peoples' deciding that they would rather not spend time in your company. Claudia suspected parents concluded "that since we don't have children, we don't like them or don't respect family values or those who have children." She wanted people to know she didn't eat little children for breakfast.

Once you do announce yourself as childless by choice, be prepared for the unexpected. Recognize that parenthood, as a choice, can sometimes be a very loaded topic, much like religion or politics, because opinions on intentional childlessness are usually informed by one or the other—or both. Most people, particularly if they are parents, have an opinion.

When I first began to out myself as childless by choice, the most unexpected response I got from parents was "That was a very smart decision," followed by confessions that they had, at times, regretted their decision to have kids. Up until I started getting this reaction, I was under the impression that all parents were happy with their lot in life. So I was surprised how often I heard it, until I started my research on this project and read about Dr. Phil's survey of parents.

So now, when I encounter parents who appear to be envious of my childfree life, I understand. But being envied is awkward. "You have it so easy," they'll say, as if all life's problems stem from parenthood and the childfree are somehow exempt from all cares and worries by virtue of their childlessness.

Madelyn Cain, author of *The Childless Revolution,* noted the "myriad of benefits" that childless women mentioned to her, including freedom from financial, emotional, and time pressures. Yet she also noted that a negative view of childless couples who enjoy these benefits persists. "How ironic," she wrote, "that we support the notion that retired people should travel and enjoy themselves, yet we reject the idea of a younger couple doing so."[14]

Sometimes I feel the impulse to tell people that they, too, could have made this choice, but I keep quiet because I understand there's no turning the clock back on parenting, and I have encountered more than a few parents who believe that parenthood was imposed on them or that other options did not exist. The truth remains that in our history and our current culture, reproductive choices are limited and reproductive options are not doled out in equitable measures. Choice, whether it be where to go to school, what job to take, or whether to have five children or none, is a luxury.

After years of talking with my friends who are parents, I came to the conclusion that there likely isn't a parent alive who hasn't experienced at least a pang of self-doubt about their choice or their ability to parent. So defensiveness is a common reaction when someone talks about choosing to be childfree. Children have a way of making us feel inadequate at times. They are idealists by nature—and so are many of the childfree, who sincerely hope that one day the choice to remain childless will be a respected, easily accessible option for anyone who wants it.

THE DOWNSIDES OF CHOOSING A
LIFE WITHOUT KIDS

Among the couples I interviewed, many had trouble identifying the downsides based on their experience alone. However, recurring themes did emerge, most of which had to do with a lack of childfree peer groups and with end-of-life challenges.

Social Isolation

Couples who identified social isolation as a disadvantage mourned the loss of friends who had had kids and then "disappeared" from the childless couples' lives. Jerry was in his thirties when he began to loose touch with friends who became parents. "They were just so busy that they didn't have the time or the room in their life for me. And they didn't feel the loss as much as I did because they were making new friends through their kids. The soccer moms would get together, the hockey dads would get together, the piano parents would get together."

Wayne told me, "Our friends had kids early, so our social circle became very small very quickly. And it's hard; even though you remain friends, you share less in common because their goals become such that their kids are first, and rightfully so."

Sylvia did not experience this until she was older and found herself in a workplace populated by parents. "I guess I never realized until recently what a liability not having children has become. I do not have anything in common with other women," she told me. At work or in a group of women, "the subject always turns to one's children or grandchildren, at which time I am totally left out of any conversation and wind up sitting silently while they all have a nice chat. Since I'm an only child, I don't even have nieces and nephews to talk about. I have no gossip."

Jennifer thought her sense of isolation had more to do with a lack of understanding. "I do feel isolated—I feel like all my friends want kids or have kids, and I can't totally understand that choice, and they can't totally understand my choice. So that is isolating in itself."

End-of-Life Concerns

The issue of what happens toward the end of life came up in my interviews with couples because I made a point of asking people, "What happens when you get old? Any fears around that?" or, "When you imagine yourself as a childfree senior, what do you imagine?" As we saw in the couples' profiles in Chapter 5, some people did express concerns about elder care, but most had addressed their fears proactively.

They were anticipating or planning for end-of-life issues, by considering long-term-care insurance plans or saving for the inevitable move to an assisted-living center. Only a few worried about being alone, as most trusted that their social networks and their planning would ensure that there would be voluntary or paid companions for them when the time came. Many couples I spoke with also had planned their response to people's assertion that later in life, they would regret their decision to remain childless. They doubted it would happen, but if they did feel regret, they had considered the possibility of mentoring or providing foster care for kids, or focusing their attention on adults in need.

Theresa couldn't come up with a downside to being child-free; her only fear around the decision was what was going to happen when she got really old, though she thought that problems associated with aging are not limited to the childfree. "Not having someone around to take care of me scares me a bit, but I'm not going to breed a caregiver. Who's to say they would even care? There are far too many old people sitting in long-term-care facilities, waiting for their children to come, and they never do."

Finding a Mate

For the single childfree person, dating—already a minefield of dos and don'ts—can present another challenge: At what point do you tell the person you're dating that you don't want children? The overwhelming responses from the childless by choice were: as soon as possible; whenever you get the op-portunity; just do it.

Theresa remembers how she felt when Darrin (now her husband) expressed his desire to remain childless. "It was on our second date," she told me. "He brought it up. I can't remember exactly what was said, but I do remember feeling this huge relief to find out that he didn't want kids, either. He was the first man to tell me he didn't want kids." In previous relationships she'd had, Theresa had made it clear early on that she did not want children. "And I was not go-ing to change my mind," she said. "This was cause for con-cern for many men because the topic came up so early, and I was often dumped shortly afterwards, either because the man did want kids or because he was scared off by the topic of conversation."

Theresa had come to realize her childfree status was a deal breaker for many men, and yet she felt it was unfair to either party to hide this very important fact. "If Darrin had said he wanted kids, I would have said, 'See ya.' There's no point sticking around if your life goals don't match up. It's hard enough to find a partner you love and trust. It's a bonus to find one who agrees on one of the most important, life-altering decisions you will ever make."

Tamara confided, "I always thought I would be the one dumped for not wanting kids." However, after dating a happily childfree man and another who was sterile, she ended up with Jason, who couldn't believe his luck at finding a woman who didn't want kids. Previously, he had resigned himself to parenthood because, according to him, "finding women who don't want kids isn't the easiest thing in the world."

Parenthood Privilege

Some of the downsides people expressed were experienced in the workplace or in healthcare environments. Although Elaine expressed "no fears, no regrets, ever," she did feel the negative impact of "workplace and public policies that favor parents." She told me, "Everything from paid leaves of absence to public assistance, medical insurance, taxes, and educational financial aid policies all favor parents and don't take into account personal responsibility in terms of family size."

Sara also felt the impact of parental privilege in the workplace. "I'm one of the few who doesn't have kids, and people get to leave early to go pick their kids up, and occasionally I feel like I have to pick up a little bit of the slack."

Louis felt the impact in his wallet. "Where I work, I cannot purchase a health plan that's for just me and my spouse. I can choose me; me and children; or me, spouse, and children. That seems unfair." It's true that as a childless by choice person, you will have to pay for services and benefits you will never use; when my husband and I moved to Virginia, I was stunned to discover this. Athletic clubs, country clubs, and the YMCA all had just two choices: single membership or family membership.

Quite a few of the people I spoke with were frustrated that they are made to feel like they have to justify their decision to remain childless when parents are not similarly expected to justify their decision to procreate.

Historian Elaine Tyler May concurs: "It's a question that is never asked of parents: 'Why did you choose to have kids?' But it's as legitimate as the 'Why don't you have kids?' question. In the era of legal abortion, and legal birth control, it is a very reasonable question to ask. Why is parenthood always the default position?"[15]

Jodi saw evidence of parental privilege every time she went to the grocery store. "I feel marginalized by society sometimes, but mostly I ignore it," said Jodi. But, she went on, "the PARKING RESERVED FOR EXPECTANT MOTHERS signs piss me off the way bathtime pisses off two-year-olds. I just can't explain it."

Birth Control Issues

Jodi's other obstacle was her lack of access to sterilization, her birth control method of choice. "I started trying to get a tubal ligation when I was eighteen," Jodi recalled. "I went in for my first gynecological exam, and after the doctor handed me a prescription for birth control that I hadn't asked for, I told him I was a virgin and celibate and was planning on remaining so for the time being, but I didn't want kids, so could he tell me about sterilization options. He was dumbfounded. No one would do it—male doctors, female doctors, didn't matter. The majority of the doctors claimed their reluctance stemmed from lawsuits from women who changed their minds and sued them for giving them a tubal ligation, so I offered to sign waivers. I imagine I could have found someone to do it, but I got tired of searching and gave up for a long time."

Most sexually active, childless by choice couples choose a vasectomy over a tubal ligation because it's less problematic and less invasive. It's an almost foolproof method of contraception, with the added bonus of being, for all intents and purposes, permanent. Which is why some of the men I interviewed were forced to shop for doctors or go the extra mile to convince a doctor that a young, healthy, virile, and still childless male would choose this course.

Yell "vasectomy!" in a room full of men, and I'll bet you a bratwurst that eight out of ten will reflexively cup a hand over their gonads. Okay, that's admittedly not a very scientific way to go about measuring the reactions of the general public, but it does illustrate why doctors and others fail to understand why a childless man might want this procedure. Some men are denied, some are asked to return with a waiver signed by their wife, and most are subjected to a lecture on how difficult it may be to reverse, the underlying message being: *You may not want kids now, but you will change your mind.*

The same assumption is made when a young childfree woman, like Jodi, seeks a tubal ligation. Good luck! Doctors in some states will refuse to do the procedure on women less than twenty-five years old, *even if they already have kids.* As I write this, a young single mom I have been mentoring for years is seeking the required two signatures from doctors to override this discriminatory practice so that she can get her tubes tied right after she delivers her second child.

Lack of access to sterilization forced Jodi to be hypervigilant and took its toll on her well-being. "I've lived in constant fear of getting pregnant, despite my keeping enough contraceptives around to kill every sperm within a ten-mile radius.

Nobody asks to be born, and I while I support a woman's right to make her own choices, the termination of a pregnancy doesn't sit well with me as a choice for myself."

Another woman I interviewed, Sue, knew at age twenty-five that she wanted to remain childfree, but was required to submit to a year of counseling before her doctor would agree to give her a tubal ligation. "Even though I strongly believe it is every woman's right to have an abortion, I didn't know if I could go through with one if I accidentally got pregnant. I knew for certain that I didn't want a child or a pregnancy, so I went the tubal ligation route. I knew then that it was the right choice for me, and time has proven it was."

Some childfree women have had to wait until they suffer some gynecological crisis before their doctor would agree to perform a procedure that would render them sterile. Not only do many doctors think people will regret their decision to remain childless, but many have gone so far as to suggest that voluntarily rendering yourself sterile might devalue you as a potential mate.

An extreme example of this belief that your value as a human being is tied to your fertility occurred in Somalia and was reported on the BBC News website in 2004:

> "A hospital in the capital of Mogadishu was forced to shut for five weeks following threats to a doctor who removed a woman's womb. Dr. Bashir Sheikh said the operation had saved Mrs. Fatuma Abdulle's life because she was carrying a dead foetus. Fatuma's family sent gunmen to the SOS Hospital, saying she was as good as dead without a womb."

It was Mrs. Fatuma Abdulle's husband who had urged the doctor to do what he could to save her life. And the doctor did save her life. However, this woman's family cared not. They wanted compensation—50 camels, in fact, the traditional compensation for 'a dead woman.'"[16]

Though extreme, this scenario supports the idea that much of the resistance to intentional childlessness has to do with religious, philosophical, or biological ideologies. The mere existence of a growing childless by choice population is a challenge to people who believe procreation is instinctive, intrinsic, biological, or obligatory.

In my interviews, reports of others' resistance to or stigmatization of childfree couples varied from region to region and family to family, and depended largely on the degree to which the couple's community, family, and peers supported their decision to remain childfree and the degree to which religious, cultural, or pronatal ideology were factors in their lives.

What If?

I encountered a couple of women who acknowledged that the main downside to being childless by choice was that they would never know what it was like to be a mother. It was one experience, of the many that present themselves over a lifetime, that, by virtue of their very deliberately choosing, they had shut the door on. These were women who also valued the freedom and opportunities their childless status offered them, and they acknowledged that it was a trade-off, but they lamented that their curiosity would never be satisfied. They would never know what motherhood would have been like for them.

"The only regret I've had, and it's a weird one, is that I didn't want children," said Grace. "I wish I had wanted them and been able to engage in the whole catastrophe of life and love it the way others have. I think that would be a very rich experience, but, again, I may be idealizing it, too."

Author Susan Jeffers, a parent and author of *I'm Okay, You're a Brat,* had this to say in my interview with her: "I love the term 'childfree.' 'Childless' implies you are missing something, where 'childfree' says you are free to live a different kind of a life. Some people say they are having a child because they don't want to miss the experience. I understand that, but understand when you have a child, you are missing different experiences. You know you can have anything you want in life, but you can't have everything. Make your choice."[17]

People talk about the chasm that exists between parents and nonparents because our worlds and our priorities are so different, but what we do share are the *what ifs.* Those go both ways: *What would my life be like with children? What would my life have been like without them?*

Jennifer didn't feel like she had a choice—she was just being who she is. "I remember a gay friend of mine saying to me how painful it was sometimes to accept that he would never have the dream—picket fence, two kids, wife, suburbia—but he couldn't change who he was to accommodate that. He couldn't compromise who he was for the norm. That's how I feel—I wish I could be 'normal' and want kids, and not have to explain my choices. But I'm not willing to give up who I am, what I want out of life, in order to be 'normal.'"

Lack of Understanding and Legitimacy

Another downside—the one that prompted me to embark on the Childless by Choice Project and write this book—is how often we are misunderstood. When I asked my participants and survey respondents, "What motivated you to participate in this project?" their responses often addressed this issue head-on:

- "The negative remarks by people who don't seem to have a clue."

- "Frustration about others' attitudes."
- "Tired of judgments and misconceptions about people who choose not to procreate."
- "People need to stop assuming. People need to start respecting couples and individuals for the choices they make."

Respect is hard to come by when your path and motives are not acknowledged as legitimate—whether by family or society or mental-health professionals. Why are our true motives not perceived as valid? Sociologist and researcher Dr. Kristin Park wrote, "The persistence of pronatalism, the cultural idea of the 'superwoman' who effortlessly combines work and family life, the emerging redefinition of masculinity to include nurturant fathering, and the current centrality of 'family values' ideology raise the question of whether, especially for women, there exist any socially acceptable motives for choosing childlessness."[18]

US VERSUS THEM

Parenthood is the default in North America, and our society struggles with the concept of intentional childlessness. Those factors, plus parental privilege (born of majority privilege), often pit parents against nonparents.

A father of two teenage sons asked me, "Why are parents so defensive when it comes to this issue?" At the time I didn't know, but after years of talking to both parents and the childfree, it seems to me that we distrust the motives of the other, each camp regularly employing the "selfish" label to describe the other's reasoning.

Parents often feel empowered to speak from a "holier than thou" place because their path is the norm. Because so many parents can't imagine their life without children, many feel obligated to convert those who haven't seen the light. Stung by the judgment and evangelistic fervor of the missionary moms and dads, some of the childfree react by using terms like "breeders" when referring to those who appear to procreate without much deliberation or restraint. It remains unclear to me whether this is a retaliatory response to the "ouches" they've experienced at the hands of parents, or whether it is politically motivated, with the goal of calling attention to what they perceive as "unintentional" or "irresponsible" parenting.

I suspect that Elaine Tyler May was right when she said in my interview with her, "We have children and they create our identity, not just because we have children but because they make us into mothers and fathers, and motherhood and fatherhood are identities that carry a lot of weight in our society."[19] If you question the status of an individual, you also question that person's identity, because they are linked in many subtle ways.

Does it really come down to the divide between those who want kids and those who don't? I don't think so. It's not us versus them. Perhaps in some corners of the online world that's true, but it doesn't have to be so. There is a way to enable both parents and nonparents to coexist happily in a healthy, progressive society that seeks to grow in strength, if not in numbers. But that would require a shift in attitude, culture, and ideals, and it would require us to embrace parenthood and nonparenthood as equal choices.

THE MOST DIFFICULT QUESTION

What question do the childless by choice have the most difficulty answering? It's definitely not "Why don't you have kids?"

The question is: "Do you have kids?"

When I asked childfree couples how they typically respond to this question, many replied, "I just say no." However, these same people recognized that this was often an insufficient response.

First of all, just saying no is a conversation ender, which might be good or bad, depending on your mood or your present company. Second, it can leave the person free to make assumptions about why you don't have kids, and open you up to the very real risk that they may assume wrongly.

Through trial and error, many of the people I had interviewed had cultivated their own customized response, which hinted at some of the underlying motives or rationales, or was designed for levity or to invite further comment or inquiry.

Here are some of my favorite responses to "Do you have kids?":

- "Nah. My gene pool's pretty shallow."
- "No. If I had a kid like me, I'd have to kill him."
- "No, I'm the only child my wife has." (My husband's response.)
- "No. I like kids, I just never wanted to own one." (My response.)
- "No kids, thank you."
- "No kids, thank God."
- "We've got two furry, four-legged children."
- "No. Why? Do you need some?"
- "None, by choice. How about you?"

CHAPTER 8

A Place at the Table

It's Thanksgiving 2008. The TV in the family room is tuned to the football game. I'm uncorking the wine, and Robert is making sure it is well distributed. Colin's tending the turkey. Jim is carving the ham. Robbie is slicing the cornbread he's just baked in Grandma's special pan. Britney's stirring the gravy, and the rest of the twenty-two people gathered here are enjoying Beth's fruit and dip.

It feels warm and intimate after a chilly morning spent with five thousand other folks at the five-kilometer Drumstick Dash, benefiting our local homeless shelter. The dash, followed by a Thanksgiving meal, has become a tradition these past few years. It feels familiar, which is kind of odd given that until about eight years ago, we didn't know most of the people we're sharing a table with today.

For the past eighteen years, we have celebrated Thanksgiving without our immediate family. Robert's family is scattered across the globe. My immediate family is five hundred miles away, in Canada. Our hosts, Debra and Jim, and their two children have graciously opened their doors to us and sixteen other people—an assortment of neighbors, friends, singles, couples, families, empty-nesters, the childless by choice, and the childless by circumstance.

It feels good, expansive, and when Robbie offers the blessing, I feel truly blessed. We are free to create a tribe beyond blood and marriage, and the result is just as sweet. As I enjoy my second helping of cornbread, I can't help but think how increasingly common this assemblage is becoming across North America.

As the numbers of childless by circumstance and voluntarily childfree continue to grow, and as the education and empowerment of women around the world drive birthrates lower, we will all be adjusting to the reality of smaller families, shifting demographics, and voluntary and involuntary childlessness.

This requires us to challenge the status quo by asking the right questions and making room for new ideals and exposing dubious assumptions.

As I discovered on my journey exploring childfree partnerships, the questions always come first.

Is love enough to sustain a successful union? Apparently, yes.

Are couples instinctively or otherwise compelled or obligated to have kids? Instinctively, no. Obligated, perhaps. Many couples I interviewed felt pressured by family members and friends to have kids, but they resisted it because they believed it would be wrong to have kids just to "appease society or family."

Can couples be happy and fulfilled without children? Yes—oh, definitely, yes.

So then, is this the beginning of the end of the world as we know it? Will voluntary childlessness become the plucked thread that will unravel our societal structure? Probably not. Although we are a significant minority, we remain the minority; most people still intend to become parents one day.

So, given that the risk of voluntary extinction is remote, can we recognize the right of couples to self-select, to determine for themselves if parenthood is right for them?

Can we also appreciate that the childfree can and do contribute to the common good, as workers, volunteers, benefactors, caregivers, teachers, leaders, artists, entrepreneurs, and academics, enabled by their childfree status to harness resources—time, energy, money, creative capital—that may not be as readily available to people who are parents?

Can we consider the environmental benefits of voluntary childlessness in a throwaway, consumer culture as we see and feel the sobering impact of encroaching landfills, urban sprawl, and diminishing natural resources?

Can voluntary childfree partnerships be considered a viable pathway for human development and well-being? And can we choose this path without being sanctioned? If so, can childfree couples be integrated as "families of two" into our society?

Can we debunk the myths surrounding parenthood and nonparenthood to allow undecided couples to make informed choices, free of these false notions?

We can. Just as we have assimilated minorities—new immigrants, gays and lesbians, single-family households—over the course of our history. Just as we have moved from the idea that children are economic assets in a preindustrial world to the idea that children are a cherished luxury in times of limited resources.

When 20 percent or more of a given population remains childless by choice or by circumstance, it's time to expand our thinking and our definitions of family.

THE FEARS

Deborah wondered about the "people who feel uncomfortable with childfree folks. Why are we a threat?"

"Why is this so threatening?" asked sociologist Dr. Kristin Park. "Why should anyone care?" She had pondered this question in the course of her study on stigma management among the childless by choice.

Dr. Park could offer only one explanation, which she credited to fellow sociologist and researcher Jean Veevers. "I recall she talks about it in terms of distributive justice. Parents have to believe that all of the sacrifices they make, the things they give up for parenting, are offset by the rewards. And if you look at someone and it seems like the scale is so much more tipped toward rewards without sacrifices, it probably seems unfair."[1]

People are giving up more to parent, and raising kids has become more difficult. Long gone are the days when people could pull their eight-year-old kids out of school to work the family farm and then expect them to marry and fend for themselves by age eighteen. The costs of raising children, in terms of time, money, and emotional support, are astronomical. And there are more options and benefits, particularly for women, if someone chooses to delay or forgo having children.

As a result, there is a fear—spoken and unspoken—that if we give people permission to choose whether or not to have children, many more will choose not to.

Much of this fear stems from the anticipated or perceived consequences of a declining population. What happens when we have fewer babies and more elderly folks? Who's going to take care of us? What happens to our economy if more couples choose not to have kids?

THE POPULATION QUESTION

In October 2006, when the U.S. population reached three hundred million people, CNN showed footage of people cheering as a digital display recorded this incredible number. *Cheering for what?* I wondered.

Two years later, I experienced the same sick feeling when the infamous Durst National Debt Clock in New York City's Times Square ran out of digits when the U.S. deficit reached $10 trillion.

I was dismayed to see that neither of these events set off alarm bells in our nation's consciousness. The Durst Organization simply ordered a new clock with two extra digits, and when environmentalists used the three-million-person mark to remind us, again, of the dangers of overpopulation, they were pooh-poohed. An organization calling itself the Population Research Institute (PRI) issued a press release that read: "The United States is suffering from insufficient population growth." Steven Mosher, the president of this organization, warned, "When you see our economy and government programs such as Social Security risking bankruptcy, you can see that the United States' annual 0.9% population growth rate is not enough."[2]

It is true that the U.S. Social Security program is at risk of extinction because our shrinking working population cannot fund the growing pool of retirees. Yet most people who make it their job to anticipate these challenges dismiss the notion that having more kids is the way to solve this problem.

"It's the height of stupidity to argue that to save a program we need to have more babies," said Dr. S. Philip Morgan, who has been studying global fertility for years. "We just change the program. Our social security system is unsustainable. We have to change the way we fund social security; it can't be a pay as you go system anymore. So it seems sort of backward to say that to prop up a social program we have to encourage people to have more births."[3]

Bill McKibben believes an increase in U.S. births would cause more problems than it would solve. In his book *Maybe One: A Case for Smaller Families,* he wrote, "To stabilize the ratio of retirees to workers, U.S. fertility would have to surge to a rate of three births per woman or higher. Not only is that unlikely to happen, it also would produce a population the size of China's within a few generations. It's not *realistic.*"[4]

In Europe and parts of Asia, a decline in birthrates was initially seen as a looming economic catastrophe, but lower birthrates are seen increasingly by some government leaders and policymakers as inevitable, manageable, and even good.

In a 2008 article titled "No Babies?" Vladimir Spidla, director of employment, social affairs, and equal opportunities for the European Commission, was quoted as saying the combination of aging populations and lower birthrates "is the inevitable consequence of developments that are fundamentally positive, in particular . . . increased life expectancy and more choice over whether and when to have children."[5]

Demographers and social scientists around the world see lower birthrates as a consequence of female education and empowerment. In many of today's economies, the survival and well-being of women and their families are no longer dependent on the number of children they bear; rather, it's their ability to function as income earners that ensures both their survival and that of their children and dependents. In fact, Future Foundation predicts that by 2030, women will be the primary breadwinner in a quarter of all families.[6]

Some of the lowest birthrates today are in industrialized yet relatively traditional countries, like Spain, Italy, Portugal, and Greece. In most of these countries, children typically don't leave the family home until they marry, due to cultural norms, unemployment, and lack of affordable housing. In tough economies, the women with good, secure jobs are often reluctant to give them up to raise children, and because most of the men and women in these countries still adhere to traditional gender roles, working moms do not expect or get much help from their husbands with household- or child-related tasks.

Do fewer babies mean a bad economy? Not necessarily. Some very strong economies have tolerated low birthrates for years. In fact, countries with a high gross domestic product per capita, like China, Canada, the United Kingdom, Singapore, Australia, and Japan, have managed to do quite well with prolonged sub-replacement fertility rates.

And the United States and Mexico are certainly not at risk of a birth dearth. It's important to note that even though the U.S. crude fertility rate bottomed out at 13.9 per 1,000 women in 2002, 4.3 million babies were born in 2007.[7] This matches the post–World War II baby boom's record high of 4.3 million births, in 1957.

Canadian women, on average, are having fewer children than American and Mexican women, and a Statistics Canada report anticipates that deaths in Canada will outnumber births by the year 2020.[8] Luckily, Canada's promise of opportunity, high quality of life, and diverse population attract global migrants. Selective immigration has enabled both Canada and the United States to grow their populations. The U.S. "imports" more than one million legal immigrants each year, adding to the thirty-five million already here. In 2002, 23 percent of all U.S. births were to foreign-born women.[9]

The world's population doubled in the forty-year span from 1960 to 2000. The trend toward smaller families and childlessness will hopefully enable us to dodge the worst-case United Nations prediction of another near doubling of the world's population, from six billion in 1999 to close to eleven billion by 2050, when a plateau of population growth is anticipated.

Jason is a scientist who believes all animals and humans have an instinct to propagate the species; however, he also believes that species populations decline (in ways that could be instinctual, learned, or otherwise) when the earth can no longer support them. Most environmental experts agree that if we do not find ways to curb population growth now, we will likely see decreases in population, not due to intentional childlessness but due to disease, famine, and increases in infant mortality.

Wayne had noticed that "there's really not a shortage of people willing to have kids." He felt that there was room for people to make a choice that was right for them, and that those who choose not to have kids could act as a counterbalance to those who have them. The childless by choice would argue that it is far better for the planet and its inhabitants to allow people to choose voluntarily to remain childless, or to have one or two children, than it is to encourage multiple births in a world that is experiencing a decline in the resources that ensure health and quality of life.

THE INTENTION AND REALITY GAP

"What effect does the trend to delay marriage and child rearing have on fertility?" I asked Dr. S. Philip Morgan.

"To a large extent, fertility delayed is fertility forgone," he told me.[10] According to Dr. Morgan, postponement of marriage and childbearing is the major factor in declining births around the world. Most young women, when asked, "How many children would you like to have?" will say they want two or more. Yet, according to 2006 Census Bureau data, U.S. women aged forty to forty-four have, on average, 1.9 children. Twenty percent of this age group had no children by chance or by choice.[11]

What happens in the span of time between wanting two children and that point in your forties when you remain childless or find yourself thinking one is enough? Well, as my participants in the Childless by Choice Project pointed out, at eighteen or twenty, parenthood is an abstract idea with no immediacy attached to it. It's a cultural assumption and not much more. But by the time you're thirty-five, parenthood has a deadline attached to it—the fertility deadline. No longer is the idea of raising a family in the realm of the abstract. Suddenly it's real, and you must make choices.

Do you start looking at your significant other as a possible parent of your future child? Do you start taking prenatal vitamins and move to a bigger home, or do you refill your prescription for birth control pills?

Or get a vasectomy? Jerry recalls, "Until the age of twenty-three or twenty-four, I had every intention of getting married and having several kids, but after baby-sitting for neighbors, being a camp counselor, teaching, and having relationships with several single mothers, it was clear to me that, even though I truly like children, I wasn't really parent material and I wouldn't be happy being a parent." And so, not without some degree of struggle, Jerry had a vasectomy.

We anticipate parenthood for all, but should we? Can we? The assumption of parenthood is optimistic in a world where anywhere from 8 to 12 percent of couples experience difficulties conceiving.[12] Sterility in men is on the rise, which many attribute to environmental causes, such as exposure to pesticides and chemicals, sexually transmitted diseases, such as chlamydia, and low sperm count. In her article titled "Environmental Factor Infertility," Joanna Karpasea-Jones noted that in 1938, only 0.5 percent of men were infertile. By the 1990s, this number had risen to 12 percent.[13]

EMPTY NESTS AND FULL PLATES

Okay, so the childless by choice are not a threat to world stability, nor are we solely responsible for an inevitable and necessary global-population decline. So the next big issue to tackle is this idea that we're somehow shirking responsibility, or that we're not mature, reasonable, and responsible adults.

Earlier, I listed some childfree people who have made enormous contributions to our society through their philanthropy, industry, or art. In her book *Without Child: Challenging the Stigma of Childlessness,* Laurie Lisle pointed out that our most beloved children's books and plays—*Peter Pan, Alice in Wonderland, Mary Poppins,* and *Little Women*—were all written by the childless. Dr. Seuss was childless, too.

As a voluntarily childless writer and the biographer of childfree artist Georgia O'Keeffe, Lisle understood the challenge of making the choice between children and the creative life. "When the urge to undertake such occupations causes or contributes to a woman's childfree state, she is liable to be considered antisocial or selfish. . . . Yet if a [childfree woman] involved in a serious calling can ignore outer and inner accusations of selfishness, she may be able to achieve a kind of expression and achievement that are as generous toward her culture as any maternal gesture toward a child."[14]

I realize that not everyone who chooses to remain childfree is going to end up a famous author, painter, or inventor—or Oprah, for that matter—because we all contribute in our own ways. I am repelled by the suggestion that if I'm not contributing to society by raising my brood, I should be off finding a cure for cancer. My point is simply that if everyone in North America is expected to justify their existence, we will all come up short.

We are enough—if there is a common theme in the childfree experience, those three words might sum it up. The childless by choice couples I interviewed had ambitions, dreams, and goals like anyone else, the only difference being that raising children was not on their to-do list.

Laura Carroll interviewed over thirty couples for her book *Families of Two: Interviews with Happily Married Couples Without Children by Choice.* She observed, "Like all of us, these couples want and seek fulfilling lives. It's just that they don't believe they need to raise children to find fulfillment. For them, children are not essential to their happiness or sense of self-worth. They may see parenting as a valuable growth opportunity— just not one for them."[15]

More than a few times I heard, "My life is complete" or, "I can't imagine having children on top of everything else I do now." It wasn't just "My plate is full"; it was also, and importantly, "This is just me. This is who I am."

ARE SOME OF US NATURALLY CHILDFREE?

"My reasons to remain childfree are natural—as natural as the longing for kids. It's a feeling from my very being," said Misty. To her, choice didn't apply. It was, according to her, "as natural as my enjoyment of certain flavors or distaste for others. You don't choose the things you love or enjoy—you just discover how you feel about them."

Deborah also felt that the choice to remain childless "wasn't a choice." She told me, "I am just being who I am."

I relate to this idea that remaining childless isn't really a choice. Though it's certainly something that most of us deliberate, I believe that that's often due to the fact that it's so culturally ingrained that we *should* want this, that we have to spend time sorting out all the reasons we don't. Kevin, who admits he never enjoyed being around children, is perplexed about why some people felt compelled to challenge his and his wife's decision not to have kids: "Why should we feel forced into having children that we won't want?"

Tracie felt the same way: "I see my friends and family struggle with raising their children. I see how much time, patience, and sacrifice it takes. Why would I—why would anyone—sign up for such an undertaking if they are not passionate about it?"

Although she thought she "could enjoy being a parent in the abstract," Jacqui, who has a PhD in psychology, had concluded that she wasn't a good candidate for parenthood, and she believes that there are many people like her who need to be relieved of their obligations as future childcare providers. "We need to devise a system, similar to the one B. F. Skinner proposed in his book *Walden Two,* whereby a select and talented few are trained to be expert childcare workers, and they have high status and pay in our society. I'm joking only a little bit."

The suggestion that not everyone is parent material frightens some who imagine that some Big Brother–type authority might be empowered to choose who is allowed to parent and who is not. But what if we were invited to self-select? That would mean that those who wanted to be parents would have children, and those who didn't would opt out—or maybe they would choose to assist in raising other people's children.

I learned that although the childless by choice do not attach a special value to having their own, biological children, many of them would be quite prepared to take on the responsibilities of caring for a child if they were called upon to do so in an emergency. I also encountered a number of childfree women who expressed a willingness to donate their eggs, if someone they knew needed them. One of my survey participants wrote, "There is something wrong with my sister's eggs, and they have approached me to be a donor. Without hesitation I have agreed to this. I don't view this as my becoming a 'mother.' If I give her some of my eggs, they aren't mine. They may have my genetic stamp on them, but the child would be hers; I would be an aunt, and she would be a mom."

Several participants expressed no affinity for infants or young children but did express an affinity for older children. I felt the same way. In fact, when I went to my local Big Brothers Big Sisters office to volunteer my services as a mentor, I requested a child over the age of twelve. I have often joked that I would have been happy to be a mom if the stork could deliver a teenager.

Apparently, Jennifer's father felt the same way: "I was aware from the time I was young that my parents would have preferred to skip all the 'little kids' experiences and just jump to having adult children. Dad always said, 'I wish you were born with a high school diploma in your mouth!' Now, don't get me wrong: My parents loved me and were excellent parents— maybe better parents for me because they weren't overly adoring parents." However, Jennifer became aware, as an adult, "that my mom certainly did not have a maternal instinct, and if

she were at childbearing age today probably would have chosen to remain childless."

Are we in a new era in which we can allow individuals to
choose for themselves whether or not they will be parents?
There are laws and freedoms already in place that allow this to
happen, yet I don't see many people proposing self-selection,
even as a way to prevent future child abuse, neglect, abandonment, or divorce. Instead we imagine that everyone has the
desire, innate knowledge, personality, and skills to be a parent,
and we imagine that the parents who struggle or fail are simply
"bad" parents who chose not to apply these skills or instincts
to raising their children.

VALUING CHOICE

Choice and free will are the necessary elements of what we
call freedom. In some faiths, free will is considered a gift from
God. In most other spheres of life, choice is valued and defended as a human right ensuring self-determination and ac-
countability for all.

Safe Haven laws in the United States allow parents to
abandon newborns, no questions asked, and yet mature adults
who want to prevent pregnancies through voluntary sterilization are subjected to mandatory counseling or are turned away
by doctors.

In my interview with Dr. Park, she told me that we risk
devaluing parenthood "if we say it's so broadly available for
everyone to succeed at. If, as a society, we claim to be prochild,
we claim to love children, then we should encourage people to
reflect very carefully on being a parent—that would be a natural extension of living that belief in a full kind of way."[16]

The participants in the Childless by Choice Project had
done this. However, their communities and the families had
not always supported this process of thoughtful deliberation.

Instead, this decision making, or even the very notion of parenthood as a choice, is sometimes thought of as unnatural or wrong-headed. In a 2003 *Real Simple* essay, Molly Peacock, a childless by choice poet, wrote about how she came to some clarity about her choice at fifty-five years old: "There's a big difference between accepting your limits and selfishness. Selfishness comes from a place of blind need. But self-awareness, that place where we recognize and forgive our weaknesses and embrace our gifts, comes from hard-won perspective. In sometimes painful self-awareness, I grew to know what I really could give the world, and it wasn't kids."[17]

INITIATING THE "KID CONVERSATION"

The childfree remind us that, yes, love is enough to sustain a union, and that fulfillment can be as simple as loving what you have. In the courtship or honeymoon stage of a relationship, two is always enough, perhaps because, in the sequencing of priorities, child rearing seems far away. When both parties assume that they will become parents, they often fail to have the "kid conversation" before they marry. But having that discussion is critical, even if both people *do* want children. Knowing your timeline, how many children you might want, whether you might be considering not having children—all of this increases the chances that both people will be onboard for what happens when it happens, and, importantly, it reduces the risk of one or both spouses harboring resentment.

"If you are truly childfree, you will want a childfree mate," said Jerry of No Kidding! "Because there is nothing—nothing— that will break a relationship faster than a disagreement over the number of kids you're going to have, especially when one says zero and the other says one, two, three, or more. There is no compromise, there's no middle ground; you can't have half a child. And for some people, anything more than zero is too many."

Jerry confided, "I lost my first wife over that very issue. She decided she wanted kids. I knew that I didn't. I tried very hard to convince myself that I could be a good and happy father because I didn't want to lose her. We had a wonderful relationship except for that one conundrum that has no solution. And the more I thought about it, the more convinced I became that I would not be a good and happy father, and that having kids was not really a good option for me. So we very reluctantly went our separate ways."

Recently, I heard Marianne Williamson, author of *A Return to Love,* on her radio show counseling a woman about a troubled relationship. I heard her say, "If you want children . . ." *Yes!* I cheered, happy because she'd used the word "if."

If parents, counselors, pastors, priests, and peers would just choose certain key words over others, we could go a long way toward moving beyond the assumption of parenthood.

Instead of: "How many kids do you want?"
Substitute: "Do you want kids?"

Instead of: "When you have children . . . "
Substitute: "If you have children . . . "

When you remove the assumptions from your questions, you facilitate a more honest dialogue; you invite people to say what they feel, rather than to say what you expect to hear from them.

If rates of childlessness continue to increase because of choice, divorce, infertility, or postponement, we might soon see a day when a quarter of our population remains childless by choice or by circumstance. So why not talk about this possibility in our counseling sessions and our conversations with future spouses and partners?

In Chapter 5, we saw how grateful childless by choice couples were to be on the same page when it came to the desire to remain childfree. In a culture of postponement, with a 50 percent divorce rate, couples are asking themselves, "Should we bring a child into the mix? Are we prepared to take on this responsibility?"

For some, the answer is a definitive no; for others, it's maybe yes, maybe no. For the childfree by choice, coming to a place where they actually voice the decision not to have children is a relief, particularly when there is no apparent void to fill, no yearning for children, and no fear of regret.

But what if one person experiences that void or yearning and their partner does not feel the same way? That's an important thing to know before you exchange those vows.

Oh, he'll change his mind when the baby comes, she hopes. *Oh, when she's thirty-five, her maternal instinct will kick in,* he thinks. If you believe that, you haven't read this book, and you haven't really listened to your partner. If you believe you can change someone else's mind about something as important as parenthood, you are kidding yourself and you are not valuing choice or honoring free will.

Some of the saddest stories I heard while doing my research for the Childless by Choice Project were those of couples who assumed parenthood for themselves and their partners, and who hadn't had the "kid conversation" until it was too late. Most were couples in their thirties who'd discovered after many years together that they did not agree on the issue of children, and now faced the demise of a relationship in which they had invested all their hopes and dreams.

If this book does nothing else but encourage couples to have a "kid conversation" before marriage, I will have done my job.

MAKING A PLACE AT THE TABLE

A society that values free will and opportunities for all is not served by a culture that tells people, "You must be a parent to be respected and honored." This script will alienate more than just a few people who instinctively recoil at such an idea, and it will backfire. Kathryn said her choice to remain childless was "probably a bit of rebellion against a society that brainwashes women into thinking that children are what they want without allowing them to really think it through for themselves."

We often feel the need to reassure our parents and therapists that we really are happy to be childfree and not simply in denial, delusional, or destined for a lifetime of regret or depression. The notion that childlessness, particularly intentional childlessness, negatively impacts mental health is largely unfounded. A 2005 study titled "Clarifying the Relationship Between Parenthood and Depression," by Ranae Evenson and Robin Simon, found that "parents report significantly more emotional distress than persons who have never had children. These findings have led mental health and family scholars to conclude that persons do not derive the same emotional benefits from parenthood as they do from marriage and employment." Evenson and Simon further concluded, "Unlike other major adult social roles in the United States, parenthood does not appear to confer a mental health advantage for individuals."[18]

In her book, *Reconceiving Women: Separating Motherhood from Female Identity,* Mardy Ireland makes a case for healthy female development outside of motherhood and points out, "Male reproductive functioning and fatherhood are not the centerpieces for adult male development theory, but female reproductive capacity has become central and definitive for normative female development. Maternity has been the cornerstone of the mature adult identity for women. However, as childlessness becomes an increasingly visible option for women, the question of female identity apart from motherhood becomes increasingly difficult to disregard or pathologize."[19]

Grace, a counselor and mediator, told me, "I think any healthy lifestyle that brings joy is valid. If having children brings joy, that's valid. If someone's happy without children, that's valid, too. Most of the great spiritual teachers in the world did not have children, and no one is upset with them. Everyone thinks it's wonderful and holy to be a nun or a priest or a monk; that is the only really socially approved childfree lifestyle."

Sue, who holds a master's in counseling psychology, said, "I am astounded that, in this day and age, some young couples still feel pressured to have children they don't really want! It seems like our society should be well past that point by now. This is a very personal decision that should be left entirely up to the couple involved. Why do so many people presume to know you better than you know yourself?"

Many of the women I spoke with thought that pronatalist ideals that glorify motherhood and fatherhood do not serve us as a culture or a community. Instead, they set us up to fail and to discriminate.

"We need to look at the negative impact that pronatalist attitudes have on our culture," said Elaine. "As a society, we've examined every 'ism,' from ageism to racism, and their effects on our lives. It's time for us to drag pronatalism out of the closet and take a serious look at it, too, and how it impacts us and the lifestyle decisions we make. It saddens me that attitudes toward childless and childfree people have not changed a whit over the last two decades, as reflected in public perceptions and workplace and public policy as well."

Jodi also saw how pronatalist myths and our unwilling-ness to challenge them hurt parents: "Someone needs to stand up and say, 'Some days you will hate your kids. It's okay. Some days you will love them so much it will hurt. Being worried about being a good parent means you are a good parent. It can be scary—it's not all rainbows and lollipops.' Our society seems to be unwilling to say stuff like that, which is a shame, because I think it would reassure a lot of folks."

Tara, who looked to people with children to help her make up her own mind about whether to have a child of her own, had this to say: "Hey, back off on the 'kids are the best thing ever' rhetoric and let me hear your real story. How much work is it? What are the pains and joys? Let me tell you about mine. We need to be more open and honest about the lifestyles of the childless and with child."

Dr. Park wanted to see more support for this choice from other women: "The women's movement is sometimes a little disappointing to me. I see the movement, very appropriately, reaching out to stay-at-home mothers and working mothers and trying to validate those choices, and advocating for important family-friendly policies, but sometimes to the exclusion of other women—women who are childless by choice or by circumstance, and single women. I'd like to see women from all walks of life—single, without or with children, married or partnered, straight or gay—respect and honor each other's choices. To me, that is what the feminist movement has always been about."[20]

In so many environments and communities, the childfree remain the elephant in the room, conditionally tolerated but largely ignored. We number in the millions, but we're hidden in plain view. We are at a point now where the culture needs to wake up to the fact that a significant number of North Americans will never have children. For those of us who remain childfree by choice, it's time that we have a voice as a demographic, and that we stand up for ourselves by expressing our choice to remain childless without shame or qualification. We are without children, it's our choice, and we wouldn't have it any other way.

Choice, after all, is the other elephant in the room. Often couples just go along, oblivious to the fact that they do have a choice when it comes to parenthood. Admittedly, it's difficult, given that we live in a culture that can make it feel like we don't: It's hard to self-select or opt out; even if we try to prevent a pregnancy, we are sometimes thwarted by lack of access to reliable contraceptives or sterilization procedures. In terms of our history, reproductive choice is still relatively new, and our healthcare providers have yet to catch up.

Same with the writers and producers of our stories; they need to let go of their simplistic, shallow, one-dimensional childfree characters—the kid haters and the gleefully selfish bohemians—and craft a real character with complex motives and a few redeemable traits, resulting in a role that an A-list actor might actually want to play.

In a world that has yet to put a human face on the childless by choice demographic, gaps in the way we're perceived are too often filled by assumptions. In a world where we remain statistically invisible, we can be easily marginalized. When our motives or decision-making processes are not understood or validated, we can be excluded—or even feared.

Along with intentional single parents and same-sex partners, childfree by choice couples struggle to find their place in a society that clings to an increasingly rare model of North American family life. A household with Mom, Dad, and two kids is no longer the reality for most North Americans, and yet politicians, marketers, and policymakers package their products as if it is.

Most of the childless by choice feel conventional in all respects outside of their childfree status, and many feel strongly connected to their "families" or tribes, which include partners, parents, siblings, nieces and nephews, pets, and close friends. Invitation is increasingly replacing procreation as a way to build a tribe. Inclusion is as simple as setting another place at the table.

LAST WORDS

At the end of every interview, I asked my participants, "Is there anything else you would like people to know about you or your decision to remain childless?"

"My being childless by choice is not something that is *wrong* with me, it's an intrinsic part of how I have chosen to shape my life," said Jodi.

Trond, the daycare worker, said, "While kids may be the future of our society, we don't all have to have them."

Anthony had this to say to couples: "Make sure you are both in agreement, because if one person really wants kids and the other doesn't, that's going to be a huge issue."

Wayne hoped his involvement in this project would encourage people to "think outside the box, as cliché as that is, to see if maybe parenthood is right for you, or maybe not. And if not, understand that you can be complete, you can be fulfilled, without having kids."

Manmeet hoped we could come to "respect people's choices—that's how humanity moves forward."

If we can expand our cultural definition of "family" to include childless and childfree families, we can move forward. If we are allowed to choose what's right for us, beyond influence and the assumption of parenthood, we can be fulfilled. If we can find a partner who is on the same page, we can remain a happy family of two. If we can see the value of children, and find value in a childfree life, we can be inclusive. If we can shape a life without children, and see that it is enough, we can be whole.

If you are childless by choice, you probably already know all these things. If you are childless by circumstance, know that it is possible to have a happy and fulfilling life without biological children, even if it takes some reconciliation to get there. If you are undecided on the issue of children, I hope you will use this book as a tool for your own decision making.

Share it with your loved ones and partners. Use it to facilitate the discussions you may be delaying because they are so darn awkward to initiate. Use what you've learned here, and read more (see the Resources section at the end of the book) so that you can harness intention with eyes wide open, cultivate realistic expectations, find a partner who shares your goals and intentions, and develop the ability to ask for support when you need it.

APPENDIX A

The Childless by Choice Project
Motivation and Decision-Making Survey

STATISTICAL ANALYSIS SUMMARY

The Childless by Choice Project started with a literature review; my intent was to do the research necessary for a book, a documentary, or both. As much of the literature was dated, cited studies that were twenty to thirty years old, my need for more current and relevant data became apparent. I needed to conduct a new survey, one that fulfilled this project's needs more specifically.

During the literature review, frequently cited motives for voluntary childlessness were noted and turned into motive statements, for the purpose of creating a questionnaire. Additional motive statements were suggested by social scientists and other expert advisors. The final motive statements were supplemented with multiple choice and open-ended questions, which provided additional data for the statistical analysis and qualitative data.

PARTICIPANTS AND METHOD

By intention, all survey respondents were over age eighteen and residents of North America who self-identified as childless by choice. A few respondents were excluded when we discovered that they had intended to be parents but circumstances, outside of their control, led to their childlessness, or they had felt, for some other reason, that they had not been free to choose to have a child, even if they had wanted to. As this survey was intended to explore both the decision-making process and the motives of the childless by choice, it was critical that the respondents felt they had been afforded the freedom to choose to be parents, or not, at some point in their lives. In some cases, one or more of the open-ended questions went unanswered by respondents. However, if it was determined that this data was not essential for the purposes of the statistical analysis, incomplete questionnaires were included, provided that all other critical data was present.

Participants were solicited through word of mouth and through No Kidding! clubs across North America. Some participants volunteered to participate after seeing an article about the Childless by Choice Project in a regional newspaper that invited readers who wanted to participate to call a local telephone number. Efforts were made to include both genders, with the goal that at least 25 percent of the respondents be male and at least 50 percent be in committed heterosexual partnerships. Efforts were also made to include respondents from both rural and urban areas.

As the childless by choice demographic had been characterized previously as largely Caucasian, less inclined to religious adherence, and college educated, we made no overt attempts to represent all races, faiths, and education levels, although ultimately some respondents of this survey described themselves as Asian, Hispanic, African American, or Native American; likewise, there were participants who described themselves as

Christian, Jewish, Eastern Orthodox, Roman Catholic, atheist, spiritual, or pagan. The only demographic data that was requested and required for the statistical analysis of this survey was the respondent's age and gender.

After qualifying based on these criteria, 171 self-selected, voluntarily childless/childfree individuals (single, partnered, and married) participated in this survey, which was conducted by Laura S. Scott from November 2004 through July 2006; 121 (71 percent) of the respondents were women, and 50 (29 percent) of the respondents were men. Questionnaires were delivered and returned by email or standard mail. A few questionnaires were filled out on-site, prior to face-to-face interviews.

For the motive-related part of the questionnaire, participants were asked to rate eighteen statements reflecting frequently cited motivations for remaining childless/childfree on a Likert scale of 0 to 5, indicating the degree to which they identified with that statement or the degree to which it applied to them in the course of their decision making. A 0 rating would indicate that the motive statement was not applicable or that the respondent did not identify at all with that statement. A higher number would indicate the relative degree to which the respondent identified with the statement, with a rating of 5 indicating a very strong identification with the statement, or an acknowledgment that it is, or was, a primary motivator in the respondent's decision to remain childless.

The intent of the statistical analysis was to determine the most compelling motives for the group as a whole, and then the most compelling motives by age, gender, and decision-maker category. Statistical analysis of the raw data was provided by Dr. Charles Houston of University Consultants, in Roanoke, Virginia.

TOP SIX MOTIVATIONS TO
REMAIN CHILDLESS/CHILDFREE

The top six motivations were determined by examining both means and the dispersion of frequencies analyses, with the intent to identify the six most compelling motivation statements.

1. I love our life, our relationship, as it is, and having a child won't enhance it.*
2. I value freedom and independence.
3. I do not want to take on the responsibility of raising a child.
4. I have no desire to have a child, no maternal/paternal instinct.
5. I want to accomplish/experience things in life that would be difficult to do if I were a parent.
6. I want to focus my time and energy on my own interests, needs, or goals.

The first three motivations listed above were determined to be top motivators because they were rated a 4 or 5 on a scale of 0 to 5 by more than 70 percent of the respondents. The remaining three were rated a 4 or 5 by over 60 percent of the respondents, indicating that they were also strong motivators for the majority of the participants. All of the motivations above had a mean rating of more than 3.5.

---

* In the initial analysis of the data this "I love our life . . ." motivation was fourth in the six. However, given that 16 percent of the respondents rated this particular variable a 0, indicating it was not applicable, and that it was very likely that the majority of this percentage of respondents were single, divorced, or widowed, it became apparent that the 0 rating needed to be dropped in the analysis of this one motivation, acknowledging that unpartnered respondents could not reasonably rate this variable otherwise, as it was worded.

Indeed when we went back to the questionnaires, we noted that none of the known partnered respondents had rated this statement a 0 and we saw that some known single respondents had indeed rated this statement a 0, even though in their answers to open-ended questions they expressed being happy with their lives and with their choice to remain childless. It is interesting to note that even with the weighting of the non-applicable ratings *over 50 percent of respondents rated this motivation a 5 in the initial analysis* giving it a mean average of over 3.5 and ensuring its place in the top six.

TOP MOTIVATIONS BY GENDER
I love our life, our relationship, as it is, and having a child won't enhance it.
This was the top motivator for both the men and the women (for those respondents to whom this variable applied—see footnote); 89 percent of the men surveyed rated this statement a 4 or 5, compared with 83 percent of the women.

I value freedom and independence.
This motivator ranked second highest for women and third highest for men; 82 percent of women and 78 percent of men rated this motive statement a 4 or 5.

I do not want to take on the responsibility of raising a child.
This was the second-highest-ranked motivator for men and one of the top motivators for women; 82 percent of men rated this motivation statement a 4 or 5, compared with 70 percent of women.

I have no desire to have a child, no maternal/paternal instinct.
This was the third-highest-ranked motivator for women; 75 percent of women rated this statement a 4 or 5 (60 percent gave it a rating of 5), compared with 64 percent of men.

I want to accomplish/experience things in life that would be difficult to do if I were a parent.
A slightly higher percentage of men than women strongly identified with this motivator; 68 percent of men and 62 percent of women surveyed rated this statement a 4 or 5.

I want to focus my time and energy on my own interests, needs, or goals.
On this statement, the genders tied; 60 percent of the men and 60 percent of the women rated it a 4 or 5.

TOP MOTIVATIONS BY DECISION-MAKING CATEGORY
Participants were asked to choose a decision-making category that they most identified with from the list below:

- Early articulators: those who make the decision early in their lives, generally without influence from a significant other.
- Acquiescers: those who make the decision to be childfree primarily because their partner wants to remain childfree.
- Postponers: those who delayed having a family and ultimately decided to remain childless/childfree.
- Undecided: those who are still in the decision-making process.

In our sample of 171 participants, 113 (66 percent) as early articulators, 15 (9 percent) as acquiescers, 37 (21.5 percent) as postponers, and 6 (3.5 percent) self-identified as undecided. As our undecided sample was so small, it was excluded from this part of the analysis. The top six motivators for each group were identified by calculating the percentage of the group that had rated the statement a 4 or 5 on a scale of 0 to 5. The top six motivations in all three groups analyzed were rated a 4 or a 5 by at least 50 percent of the whole group.

- I love our life, our relationship, as it is, and having a child won't enhance it.
- I value freedom and independence.
- I do not want to take on the responsibility of raising a child.

On these three motive statements, early articulators, postponers, and acquiescers agreed: Each was rated a 4 or 5 by at least 70 percent of the respondents in each of our three categories. All (100 percent) of the acquiescers rated the "I love our life . . . " statement a 4 or 5. A large majority (84 percent) of early articulators rated "I value freedom and independence" a 4 or 5. And 76 percent of postponers rated "I do not want to take on the responsibility of raising a child" a 4 or 5.

I have no desire to have a child, no maternal/paternal instinct.
Early articulators strongly identified with this statement; 79 percent of this group rated it a 4 or a 5. The majority of postponers also identified with this statement; 65 percent of this group rated it a 4 or 5. A minority (47 percent) of acquiescers rated this statement a 4 or 5.

I want to accomplish/experience things in life that would be difficult to do if I were a parent.
Acquiescers strongly identified with this statement; 73 percent rated this statement a 4 or 5, compared with 65 percent of early articulators and 62 percent of postponers.

I want to focus my time and energy on my own interests, needs, or goals.

This was the fourth-most-compelling motivator for both the postponers and the acquiescers; 67 percent of the acquiescers and 68 of the postponers rated this statement a 4 or 5, compared with 57 percent of early articulators.

The costs outweigh the benefits, financially and otherwise.

Postponers strongly identified with this statement; 65 percent of postponers rated it a 4 or 5, compared with 54 percent of early articulators and 47 percent of acquiescers.

I delayed having children and eventually decided I wanted to remain childless.

Not surprisingly, 65 percent of postponers strongly identified with this statement, rating it a 4 or 5, compared with 27 percent of acquiescers and 7 percent of early articulators.

My partner does not want kids.

Acquiescers strongly identified with this statement; 67 percent rated it a 4 or 5, compared with 43 percent of postponers and 38 percent of early articulators.

TOP MOTIVATIONS BY AGE GROUP

- I love our life, our relationship, as it is, and having a child won't enhance it.
- I value freedom and independence.
- I do not want to take on the responsibility of raising a child.
- I have no desire to have a child, no maternal/paternal instinct.

The above motive statements were rated a 4 or 5 by over 60 percent of survey respondents in each of the following age groups:

20–29
30–39
40–49
50 and over*

The majority of the survey respondents were 30 to 49 years old; 17 (10 percent) of the respondents were 20 to 29 years old, 70 (41 percent) were 30 to 39 years old, 48 (28 percent) were aged 40 to 49, and 36 (21 percent) were over 50 when they took the survey (during the twenty months between November 2004 and July 2006).

* The 50 and over category was created, combining the 50–59 group and the 60–69 group, because there were only four respondents over the age of 60. The eldest was 66 years old.

I love our life, our relationship, as it is, and a child won't enhance it.

Over 80 percent of all age groups (for those whom this variable applied) rated this statement a 4 or 5. This was the top motivator for the 40-and-older groups; 90 percent of the 50-and-over group and 83 percent of the 40–49 group strongly identified with this statement.

I value freedom and independence.

This was the top motivator for the 20–29 group; 100 percent rated this statement a 4 or 5, compared with 61 percent of the over-50 group. It was also the top motivator for the 30–39 group; 87 percent rated it a 4 or 5.

I do not want to take on the responsibility of raising a child.

This was the third-highest-ranked motivator for the 30–39 group; 81 percent rated this motivation statement a 4 or 5. It was also the third-highest-ranked motivator for the over-50 group; 64 percent rated it a 4 or 5.

I have no desire to have a child, no maternal/paternal instinct.
This was the second-highest-ranked motivator for the 50-and-older group; 69 percent strongly identified with this statement. However, all of the age groups found this a compelling motivator; over 64 percent of all groups rated it a 4 or 5.

I want to accomplish/experience things in life that would be difficult to do if I was a parent.
This motive statement tied with the statement above as the third-highest-ranked motivator for the 40–49 group; 73 percent of this age group rated it a 4 or 5.

I want to focus my time and energy on my own interests, needs, or goals.
This statement tied with the "I do not want to take on the responsibility of raising a child" statement as the third-highest-ranked motivator for the 20–29 group; 71 percent strongly identified with this statement, compared with 42 percent of the 50-and-older group.

The costs outweigh the benefits, financially and otherwise.
Although this motive statement did not make it into the top six motives for all the age groups, it did get a 4 or 5 rating from 63 percent of respondents aged 40–49. In comparison, only 39 percent of the 50-and-over group strongly identified with this motive statement.

I am concerned about the state of our world, and I do not think it would be wise to bring a child into it.
Although this motive statement did not make it into the top six most compelling motives for the group as a whole, it proved

to be a significant motive for the 40–49 age group; 58 percent rated it a 4 or 5, compared with 29 percent of the 20–29 age group. It was also a significant motivator for the over-50 group; 46 percent of this age group strongly identified with this statement, ensuring its place in the top six most compelling motives for this age group.

INTENT AND CONCLUSIONS

The intent of the survey was to provide contemporary data to be utilized in the research for the Childless by Choice Project, and by future researchers, and to employ both qualitative and quantitative data to determine the most compelling motives for voluntary childlessness and explore the decision-making process. Much of what we have summarized here relates to motives, as much of the qualitative data relating to the decision-making process did not lend itself to conventional statistical analysis.

The Childless by Choice Project motivation and decision-making survey yielded data that can be useful in substantiating findings of previous studies on motives of the childless by choice. The top six most compelling motives for this sample of 171 respondents are comparable to motives or rationales cited in North American and British studies and literature, including but not limited to the work done by Jean Veevers (1973), Sharon Houseknecht (1987), Fiona McAllister and Lynda Clarke (1998), Patricia Lunnenborg (2000), and Kristin Park (2005). Some motives cited as compelling or frequent in previous studies, such as career considerations for women and dislike of children, were not substantiated as the most compelling motives for the Childless by Choice Project respondents as a whole. Data from this survey also suggests that environmental concerns or the population-growth motive (expressed most often in this survey as the motive "I can better serve the world by not having children") may be less of a consideration for this contemporary sample of the voluntarily childless; only 46 percent of the respondents strongly identified with this motive statement.

Although respondents in this survey were invited to add motives to the list of eighteen motive statements presented in the questionnaire, very few respondents did so, suggesting that the motive statements used in the questionnaire reflect a fairly complete range of motives for voluntary childlessness.

This survey and the subsequent interviews with a smaller sample of participants (composed mostly of heterosexual couples) have exposed opportunities for future research and the need for a more expansive definition of the childless by choice, without restrictions based on the age at which they made this decision. Qualitative findings suggest that the decision making may span up to fifteen years, even for those who self-identify as early articulators. It appears that the influence of pronatalist ideology may impede or delay actions that reflect the intent to remain childless, and may prompt couples to delay decision making until a point when they can challenge pronatalist norms and expectations more comfortably. The qualitative data also suggests that more research about the influence of personality traits on the decision making, as well as about the underlying assumptions and belief systems that buttress the rationales for voluntary childlessness, is needed.

TO THE READER AND RESEARCHER

I want to remind you again that the intent of this survey was to provide contemporary data to be utilized in my study of individuals who are childless by choice, and to share its findings with the readers of this book. In addition, I am hoping that this project, including the research methods and questionnaire, can provide more data and designs for future researchers seeking to employ both qualitative and quantitative data in determining the motives for voluntary childlessness and in exploring the decision-making processes. I encourage you to freely use my research methods and design, including the questionnaire, but I would request that you cite this work and contact me through my publisher or through the Childless by Choice Project web-site (www.childlessbychoiceproject.com), so that I may review your work to increase my knowledge and understanding of the scope and extent of new research on the childless by choice.

APPENDIX B

The Childless by Choice Project
Survey Questionnaire

The survey questionnaire originally came in two parts. Part one was a description of the Childless by Choice Project and its intent, followed by some questions designed to obtain the participants' background and contact information, and to qualify them. All participants were asked to choose from three levels of participation: to participate in the survey only; to participate in the survey and be interviewed for the book (in which they had the option to choose pseudonyms); or to participate fully, meaning that they would participate in the survey and agree to a video interview for possible use in the documentary (the full-participation option was limited to couples in committed partnerships).

Part two of the questionnaire, which appears below, is the questionnaire from which we gathered the data for the Childless by Choice Project survey analysis. In cases in which the person expressed a desire to participate in the book or documentary, this questionnaire was supplemented by a face-to-face, phone, or email interview, with questions pulled from a menu designed to more fully explore the decision-making process and the rationales behind the person's choice to remain childfree.

Part two went through some modifications over the two years we conducted the survey, but this version is the most complete and best represents the questionnaire that the majority of the respondents were asked to complete.

QUESTIONNAIRE TWO: MOTIVATIONS AND DECISION MAKING

1. What motivated you to remain childless?

Please rate the following statements, on a sliding scale from 0–5, to the degree to which you identify with that statement or the degree to which it applied to you in the course of your decision making. Use a rating of zero to indicate that statement is not applicable to you or you do not identify at all with that particular statement. A rating of 5 would indicate that you very strongly identify with that statement and it is, or was, a primary motivation in your decision to be childless.

RATING:

_____ My lifestyle/career is incompatible with raising children.

_____ I value freedom and independence.

_____ I can serve myself better by not having children.

_____ I can better serve the world by not having children.

_____ I have no desire to have a child, no maternal/paternal instinct.

_____ The costs outweigh the benefits, financially and otherwise.

_____ I don't think I would make a good parent.

_____ I don't enjoy being around children.

_____ I am concerned about the physical risks of childbirth and recovery.

_____ I have seen or experienced firsthand the effects of bad or unintentional parenting, and I don't want to risk the chance that I might perpetuate that situation.

_____ My partner does not want kids.

_____ I love our life, our relationship, as it is, and having a child won't enhance it.

_____ I delayed having children and eventually decided I wanted to remain childless.

_____ I want to focus my time and energy on my own interests, needs, or goals.

_____ I do not want to take on the responsibility of raising a child.

_____ I want to accomplish/experience things in life that would be difficult to do if I were a parent.

_____ I am concerned about the state of our world, and I do not think it would be wise to bring a child into it.

_____ People I know have not realized the rewards they expected as a parent.

In the space below, please add and rate any other motivations that apply to you but are not listed above.

RATING:

_____

_____

2. Which of the above are, or were, the two most compelling motivators for you? Please elaborate.

_____
_____
_____
_____
_____
_____
_____
_____
_____

3. Can you recall any particular events or defining moments in your life that influenced your decision to remain childless?

_____
_____
_____
_____
_____
_____
_____
_____
_____

4. To help me to further understand what influenced or guided your decision to be childless, please complete the following statement:

I chose/choose to remain childfree because I believe:

_____

_____

_____

_____

_____

_____

5. Sociologists and researchers have determined that the childless by choice generally fall into four categories, depending on how they came to the decision to be childfree.

- Early articulators are those who make the decision early in their lives, generally without influence from a significant other.
- Acquiescers are those who make the decision to be childfree primarily because their partner wanted to be childfree.
- Postponers are those who delayed having a family and ultimately decided they didn't want kids.
- Undecided are those who are still in the decision-making process.

Which category do you most identify with?

_____

6. Let's create a parenthood test!
In your opinion, what questions should undecided couples ask themselves prior to making the decision to have kids or not to have kids?

_____

_____

_____

_____

_____

_____

_____

_____

_____

_____

_____

7. Name*: _____

Age: _____

Sex: _____

*If you would like to remain anonymous, your first name and the first initial of your last name is sufficient.

If you would like to be informed of the progress of this project and the results of the survey, please add your email address here:

_____

_____

_____

_____

_____

_____

NOTES

CHAPTER 1. WHO ARE THE CHILDLESS BY CHOICE?

1. Barbara Downs, "Fertility of American Women: June 2002," U.S. Census Bureau, 2003, www.census.gov/prod/2003pubs/p20-548.pdf (accessed October 20, 2008).

2. Statistics Canada, General Social Survey Cycle 15, *Family History,* 2001.

3. Kristin Park, "Choosing Childlessness: Weber's Typology of Action and Motives of the Voluntarily Childless," *Sociological Inquiry* 75, no. 3 (2005): 372–402.

4. Sylvia Ann Hewlett, Carolyn Buck Luce, Peggy Shiller, and Sandra Southwell, "High-Achieving Women, 2001," Center for Work-Life Policy/National Parenting Association, 2002.

5. T. J. Mathews and Brady E. Hamilton, "Mean Age of Mother, 1970 to 2000," Center for Health Statistics Reports, Volume 51, Number 1 (2002). www.cdc.gov/nchs/data/nvsr/nvsr51/nvsr51_01.pdf

6. U.S. National Center for Health Statistics, "Births: Final Data for 2005," www.cdc.gov/nchs/fastats/births.htm; "Trends in Canadian and American fertility," *Daily,* July 3, 2002, Statistics Canada.

7. S. Philip Morgan, interview by author, Durham, NC, July 17, 2006.

8. Susan Stobert and Anna Kemeny, "Childfree by Choice," *Canadian Social Trends,* summer 2003, www.statcan.gc.ca/kits-trousses/pdf/social/edu04_0030a-eng.pdf.

9. Tara Regan, "Emerging Adulthood," Abt SRBI Newsroom, November 5, 2004, www.srbi.com/time_emerging_adulthood.html.

10. Barbara Dafoe Whitehead and David Popenoe, "The State of Our Unions: The Social Health of Marriage in America," National Marriage Project, 2003, http://marriage.rutgers.edu/Publications/SOOU/TEXT-SOOU2003.htm.

11. Czech demographer Tomas Sobotka, speaking on European fertility trends at the Vienna Institute of Demography conference in Brussels in February 2007, concluded that low fertility rates were likely temporary due to postponement, and that "replacement migration" (meaning immigration) could serve as a counterbalance.

CHAPTER 2. THE DAWNING OF CHOICE

1. Elaine Tyler May, interview by author, Richmond, VA, April 2, 2008.

2. Elaine Tyler May, *Barren in the Promised Land: Childless Americans and the Pursuit of Happiness* (New York: Basic Books, 1995), 50.

3. Ibid., 131.

4. Betty Friedan, *The Feminine Mystique* (New York: W. W. Norton, 1997), 69–70.

5. University of Michigan, "Population Growth over Human History," University of Michigan's Global Change Curriculum, 2006, www.globalchange.umich.edu (accessed December 15, 2008).

6. Judith R. Seltzer, *The Origins and Evolution of Family Planning Programs in Developing Countries* (Santa Monica, CA: Rand, 2002), 13.

7. David Canning, "Comment on Projected Economic Growth in China and India the Role of Demographic Change," Asian Development Bank, 2006, www.adb.org (accessed December 15, 2008).

8. U.S. Supreme Court, *Griswold v. Connecticut,* 381 U.S. 479 (1965), Find-Law, http://caselaw.lp.findlaw.com (accessed December 15, 2008).

9. Christabelle Sethna, "The Evolution of the Birth Control Handbook: From Student Peer-Education Manual to Feminist Self-empowerment Text, 1968–1975," CBMH/BCHM 23, no.1 (2006): 89–118.

10. Ellen Peck, *The Baby Trap* (New York: Pinnacle, 1972), 247.

11. Park, "Choosing Childlessness."

12. "Births, Marriages, Divorces, and Deaths: Provisional Data for January 2008," National Vital Statistics Report 57, no. 3 http://www.cdc.gov/nchc/data/nvsr/nvsr57/nvsr57_03.pdf.

13. Sharon R. Cohany and Emy Sok, "Trends in Labor Force Participation of Married Mothers of Infants." *Monthly Labor Review,* February 2007.

14. U.S. Census Bureau, "Father's Day: June 18," Facts for Features press release, 2006, (accessed October 20, 2008).

15. Barbara Risman, interview by author, Raleigh, NC, February 17, 2005.

16. Stephanie Mencimer, "The Baby Boycott," *Washington Monthly,* June 2001, www.washingtonmonthly.com/features/2001/0106.mencimer.html (accessed December 15, 2008).

CHAPTER 3. ASSUMPTION, DECISION, OR SOMETHING IN BETWEEN?

1. Kristin Park, interview by author, New Wilmington, PA, June 8, 2005.

2. Jeanne Safer, *Beyond Motherhood: Choosing a Life Without Children* (New York: Pocket Books, 1996), 87.

CHAPTER 4: EIGHTEEN REASONS (AND MORE) WHY WE DON'T HAVE KIDS

1. M. Elias, "Couples in Pre-Kid, No-Kid Marriages Happiest," *USA Today,* August 12, 1997, 1D.

2. Sharon K. Houseknecht, "Childlessness and Marital Adjustment," *Journal of Marriage and Family* 41, no. 2 (1979): 259–65.

3. Judith Warner, "I Love Him, I Love Him Not," *New York Times,* February 14, 2005.

4. Vincent Ciaccio, "Summary of Thesis," Child-free.com, http://cfsurvey.freeservers.com/SummaryofThesis.htm (accessed January 20, 2008).

5. Laurie Lisle, *Without Child: Challenging the Stigma of Childlessness* (Florence, KY: Routledge, 1999), 160.

6. Park, "Choosing Childlessness."

7. Steve Farkas, Jean Johnson, and Ann Duffett with Leslie Wilson and Jackie Vine, "A Lot Easier Said Than Done: Parents Talk About Raising Children in Today's America," report prepared for State Farm Insurance

Companies by Public Agenda, www.publicagenda.org/citizen/research-studies/children-families.

8. Park, interview by author.

9. Laurie Lisle, *Without Child: Challenging the Stigma of Childlessness* (New York: Routledge, 1999), 137.

10. Vincent Ciaccio, "Summary of Thesis," Child-free.com, http://cfsurvey. freeservers.com/SummaryofThesis.htm (accessed January 20, 2008).

11. Madelyn Cain, *The Childless Revolution: What It Means to Be Childless Today* (Cambridge: Da Capo Press, 2002), 110.

CHAPTER 5. ON THE SAME PAGE: SOUL MATES, PARTNERS, AND BEST FRIENDS

1. Safer, *Beyond Motherhood,* 127.

CHAPTER 6. MARGINAL AND MISUNDERSTOOD: THE MYTHS AND REALITIES OF LIVING CHILDFREE

1. *Webster's New Collegiate Dictionary* (Springfield, MA: G. & C. Merriam Company, 1980), 697.

2. Fiona McAllister and Lynda Clarke, "Choosing Childlessness," Family Policy Studies Centre and Joseph Rowntree Foundation, 1998.

3. Park, "Choosing Childlessness."

4. Ronnie Friedland, "Family Members as Caregivers: Pros and Cons, Rights and Reimbursements," Care.com, www.care.com/child-care-a01171501-family-members-as-caregivers-pros-and-cons-rights-and-reimbursements.html.

5. Sherryl Jeffries and Candace Konnert, "Regret and Psychological Well-being Among Voluntarily and Involuntarily Childless Women and Mothers," *International Journal of Aging and Human Development* 54, no. 2 (2002): 89–106.

6. Martha Smilgis and Christine Gorman and Bill Johnson, "Here Come the DINKs," April 20, 1987, *Time,* www.time.com/time/magazine/article/0,9171,964062,00.html.

7. Steve Sailer, "Bad Schools, Immigration, and the Great Middle-Class Massacre," Vdare.com, September 28, 2003, www.vdare.com/Sailer/two_incomes.htm.

8. "Nebraska Safe-Haven Law better with Age Cap," *News Record,* January 11, 2009, www.newsrecord.org/sections/opinion/nebraska_safe-haven_law_better_with_age_cap.

CHAPTER 7. CHILDLESS IN BABYVILLE: NAVIGATING A PRONATALIST WORLD

1. Leslie Lafayette, *Why Don't You Have Kids?: Living a Full Life Without Parenthood* (New York: Kensington Books, 1995), 18.

2. "The Question of Contraceptives: A Lecture Delivered to Some Clergy of the Diocese of Manchester," *Theology,* December 16, 1930, http://anglicanhistory.org/england/goudge1930.html (accessed December 16, 2008).

3. Pew Research Center for the People & the Press, "Beyond Red vs. Blue," May 25, 2005, http://people-press.org/report/?pageid=945 (accessed January 16, 2008).

4. Arthur C. Brooks, "The Fertility Gap," *Wall Street Journal Digital Network,* August 22, 2006, www.opinionjournal.com/editorial/feature.html?id=110008831 (accessed January 16, 2008).

5. Morgan, interview by author.

6. Population Division, Department of Economic and Social Affairs, "World Population Prospects: The 2002 Revision," *POPULATION Newsletter,* December 2002, www.un.org/esa/population/publications/popnews/News74.pdf.

7. Joe McAllister, "Baby Not on Board," *News of Delaware County,* April 5, 2007, www.50reasons.com/reviews.html. (This quote was from an interview with the author, not from the book itself.)

8. Transcript from *Meet the Press,* December 26, 2004, www.msnbc.msn.com/id/6755915.

9. Lisa De Moraes, "'Family First' and the First Family," *Washington Post,* September 30, 2004, www.washingtonpost.com/wp-dyn/articles/A61075-2004Sep29.html.

10. Laurence Bergreen, *Louis Armstrong: An Extravagant Life* (New York: Broadway Books, 1997), 491.

11. Transcript from *60 Minutes,* "The Dame: Helen Mirren," February 25, 2007, http://sixtyminutes.ninemsn.com.au/article.aspx?id=259488.

12. Helen Mirren, *In the Frame: My Life in Words and Pictures* (New York: Atria Books, 2007), 254.

13. Morgan, interview by author.

14. Madelyn Cain, *The Childless Revolution: What It Means to Be Childless Today* (Cambridge, MA: Da Capo Press, 2002), 141.

15. May, interview by author.

16. *BBC News,* "Is a Woman Only Worth Her Children?" June 4, 2004, http://news.bbc.co.uk/2/hi/africa/3774827.stm.

17. Susan Jeffers, interview by author, Santa Monica, CA, January 26, 2005.

18. Park, "Choosing Childlessness."

19. May, interview by author.

CHAPTER 8. A PLACE AT THE TABLE

1. Park, interview by author.

2. Population Research Institute, "Population Group Says 300 Million Americans Is Not Enough," press release, 2006, http://pop.org (accessed December 1, 2008).

3. Morgan, interview by author.

4. Bill McKibben, *Maybe One: A Case for Smaller Families* (New York: Plume, 1999), 146.

5. Russell Shorto, "No Babies?" *New York Times,* June 29, 2008, www.nytimes.com/2008/06/29/magazine/29Birth-t.html?_r=1 (accessed July 30, 2008).

6. Steve Doughty, "Women to Be the Major Breadwinners in a Quarter of Families by 2030," *Mail Online,* August 3, 2007, www.dailymail.co.uk/news/article-472784/Women-major-breadwinners-quarter-families-2030.html.

7. National Center for Health Statistics, "Births, Marriages, Divorces, and Deaths: Provisional Data for January 2008," *National Vital Statistics Report*

57, no. 3, August 21, 2008, www.cdc.gov/nchs/ (accessed December 3, 2008).

8. Statistics Canada, "Canada Population Future," September 7, 2007, (accessed December 3, 2008).

9. *WorldNetDaily,* "Births to Immigrants at All-Time High," July 8, 2005, www.worldnetdaily.com (accessed December 2, 2008).

10. Morgan, interview by author.

11. Jane Lawler Dye, "Fertility of American Women: 2006," Current Population Reports, August 2008, www.census.gov (accessed November 10, 2008).

12. *Reproductive Health Outlook,* "Infertility. Overview/Lessons Learned," 2002, www.rho.org (accessed December 10, 2008).

13. Joanna Karpasea-Jones, "Environmental Factor Infertility," Suite101 .com, February 24, 2007, http://infertility.suite101.com/article.cfm/environmental_factor_infertility.

14. Lisle, *Without Child,* 196.

15. Laura Carroll, *Families of Two: Interviews with Happily Married Couples without Children by Choice* (Philadelphia: Xlibris, 2000), 17.

16. Park, interview by author.

17. Molly Peacock, "Life Lessons," *Real Simple* (May 2003): 207.

18. Ranae Evenson and Robin Simon, "Clarifying the Relationship Between Parenthood and Depression," *Journal of Health and Social Behavior* 46, no. 4 (December 2005): 341–58.

19. Mardy Ireland, *Reconceiving Women: Separating Motherhood from Female Identity* (New York: Guilford Press, 1993), 7.

20. Park, interview by author.

RESOURCES

BOOKS FOR THE CHILDLESS AND CHILDFREE

A good number of books have been written on this topic, but some are now out of print or difficult to find in local bookstores. Below, I've listed a few of the most popular books that have been published in the last ten years. You can find a more complete list by searching Amazon.com, where you can find new, used, and out-of-print books. It was on Amazon that I found Leslie Lafayette's book *Why Don't You Have Kids?: Living a Full Life Without Parenthood,* which is a classic and one of my favorites; sadly, this book is out of print, but it is still available online.

The Childless Revolution: What It Means to Be Childless Today, by Madelyn Cain. Published by Da Capo Press, 2002. This book explores childlessness in all its expressions, devoting only one chapter to the childless by choice. However, if you are childless by circumstance, you will likely find a story similar to yours here, as well as encouragement to challenge some of the misconceptions about childlessness.

The Chosen Lives of Childfree Men, by Patricia Lunneborg. Published by Bergin & Garvey, 1999. This book explores the choice to be childfree from an exclusively male perspective. Excerpts of interviews with thirty American and British men are grouped by motivation and ideals.

Nobody's Mother: Life Without Kids, edited by Lynne Van Luven. Published by TouchWood Editions, 2006. This is a collection of essays written by women who are intentionally childfree or childless by circumstance and have embraced a life without biological children. The sequel, *Nobody's Father: Life Without Kids,* edited by Van Luven and Bruce Gillespie, was published in 2008.

BOOKS FOR THE UNDECIDED

Do I Want to Be a Mom?: A Woman's Guide to the Decision of a Lifetime, by Diana L. Dell and Suzan Erem. Published by McGraw-Hill, 2003. This book combines expert information, decision-making tools, and anecdotes both from women who have chosen motherhood and from women who have chosen to be childfree.

I'm Okay, You're a Brat!: Setting the Priorities Straight and Freeing You from the Guilt and Mad Myths of Parenthood, by Susan Jeffers. Published by Renaissance Books, 2001. This book serves both guilt-plagued parents and the undecided by honestly exploring the pitfalls and the myths of parenthood, acknowledging that parenthood is not always as advertised, nor is it for everyone.

The Parenthood Decision: Discovering Whether You Are Ready and Willing to Become a Parent, by Beverly Engel. Published by Main Street Books, 1998. The author, a licensed marriage counselor, provides short questionnaires designed to help potential parents decide whether they are ready, willing, and able to parent. If they are not, Engel supports the childless option, stating, "You owe it . . . to your future baby to make your decision based on reality, not fantasy."

AFFINITY GROUPS

Childfree Meetup Groups are regional social groups that function independently. When I wrote this, there were fifty-two Childfree Meetup Groups in three countries. Check the website to find a group in your area.
www.childfree.meetup.com

Childfree_Singles is a Yahoo! group dedicated to bringing together like-minded childfree singles. You will have to join this online group to participate.
www.groups.yahoo.com/group/childfree_singles

I Do NOT Want Kids is a free dating site for singles who do not have children and do not intend to have them. You must register on the website to send and receive messages and post photos.
www.puzzele.com/datingsite/index.php

No Kidding! is an international social club for childfree and childless couples and singles. Check the website to find clubs in your area or information on how to start a club.
www.nokidding.net

WEBSITES

Many websites have been created by and for the childless by choice. To find them, type "childfree" or "childless by choice" into the search field of your favorite online search engine.

You can also go to the Childfree-by-Choice Pages, a site that functions as a "clearinghouse of childfree-by-choice information" by providing a good list of books and links to other childfree-focused websites.
www.childfree.net/index.html

Wikipedia has a childfree page that offers some information on the motives, history, and some of the controversy surrounding people's choice to remain childfree. This page also includes a reference and reading section.
www.en.wikipedia.org/wiki/Childfree

The Childless by Choice Project also has a dedicated website that includes information on the book, the documentary, and the survey, as well as a blog.
www.childlessbychoiceproject.com

Why Is It So Important For You to Have a Baby? This is a questionnaire specifically for people who would like to explore their motives and ideals around parenthood. It is a clever tool with which to launch a discussion with your partner if you are still undecided or ambivalent about parenthood.
www.childfree.net/potpourri_whybaby.html

ABOUT THE AUTHOR

Laura S. Scott enjoyed a career in fashion, publishing, and consulting prior to embarking on the Childless by Choice Project. In between projects, she writes screenplays, essays, and travel pieces and contributes to blogs and ezines, including www.childlessbychoiceproject.blogspot.com and www.unscriptedlife.net.

Scott nests in southwest Virginia but is equally at home traveling the world with her husband, Robert.

© Amy Nance

ACKNOWLEDGMENTS

Nonfiction books are often a response to a question. This was true for this book, too. At the beginning of my research on the Childless by Choice Project, I had questions; so did my survey participants and others I spoke with about this project.

I extend a thank-you to all those who asked the right questions, and to so many others who provided the answers, or the clues that drove me to investigate further.

My first thank-you goes to all those who participated in this project, either as survey respondents or as interview subjects, or both. They entrusted me with their stories and their motives, or they shared their ideas and their expertise, and for that I am truly grateful.

I would also like to acknowledge those who came before me: those researchers and investigators who have sought to more fully explore the rationales behind the choice to remain childfree, and those who suggested that this might be more than just a lifestyle choice.

Heaps of thanks and gratitude go to my advisors on this project, who offered their knowledge, support, encouragement, and suggestions: Dr. LeeRay Costa, James Crawford, the Honorable Martha Farnsworth-Riche, Dr. Rita Krasnow, Dr. Kristin Park, Dr. Barbara Risman, and Dr. Debra Thorne. A special thank-you goes to Dr. Charles (Chas) Houston, who assisted me in analyzing my survey data, and to Jerry Steinberg and Laura and Vincent Ciaccio, the founder of and spokespeople for No Kidding!, respectively, for their advice and help.

Thanks also to the members of No Kidding! clubs across North America who welcomed my videographer, Robert Smith, and me at the 2005 No Kidding! Convention and offered their participation, stories, and support.

To those who offered their precious time to transcribe interviews—Cynthia Anselmi, Mary Bishop, Lisa Brooks, Karen Chase, Kathy Durbin, Sylvia Fox, Sara Hanson, Sandra Kelly, Lorna Lippa, Blake Lipscomb, Sharon Mullen, Amy Rhodes, Andrew Scott, Ron Weeks—I cannot thank you enough. I could not have done this enormous task alone.

To my dear writer and filmmaker friends, and members of BRADS, FUMA, and the Southern Documentary Fund—you know who you are—much appreciation for the valued critiques and camaraderie. And to Robert Smith and Derek Anderson, many thanks for the company and the expertise on, and off, the Childless by Choice Project road trips.

To my interns, Michelle Nerling, Amy Rhodes, and Sera Tabb, I send my thanks and best wishes for what I trust will be bright futures and more rewarding ventures.

Big hugs go to my friends, listeners, and readers, a long list that includes Linda Booker, Nancy Canestrari, Claudia Cardillo, Karen Chase, Karen Clark, Marilyn Donato, Edrie Greer, Ibby Greer, Linda Habermann, Carolyn Kwiatkowski, Lorna Lippa, Kristina Menezes, and Debra Vascik. Thank you for your encouragement and support during this project, and for your friendship.

Unending thanks go to my family members, who support me in whatever I do: my husband, Robert Scott, my parents, Else and Doug Weeks, and my brother, Ron. And to my cousins, Dennis, Darren, and George, a special thank-you for hosting me during my Childless by Choice Project travels.

Heaps of gratitude and acknowledgment go to my editor, Brooke Warner, and the team at Seal Press, who rescued my proposal from the slush pile and helped me chisel a book out of blocks of text.

A final acknowledgment goes to all those who are building a life without biological children, outside of the norm and beyond the assumption of parenthood. Thank you for clearing a pathway for all who come after.